The Bumper
Scottish
JOKE BOOK

First published in 2006
by
Appletree Press Ltd
The Old Potato Station
14 Howard Street South
Belfast, BT7 1AP

Tel: +44 (0) 28 90 24 30 74
Fax: + 44 (0) 28 90 24 67 56
E-mail: reception@appletree.ie
Web-site: www.appletree.ie

A catalogue record for this book is available from the British Library.

The Bumper Scottish Joke Book

ISBN-13: 978 0 86281 987-3
ISBN-10: 0 86281 987-3

Desk & Marketing Editor: Jean Brown
Editor: Jim Black
Design: Stuart Wilkinson
Production Manager: Paul McAvoy
Cover illustration: Victoria Stothard

9 8 7 6 5 4 3 2 1

AP3328

Dedicated to Scotsmen and Scotswomen all over the world.

The Bumper Scottish JOKE BOOK

APPLETREE PRESS

Written by Terry Adlam

A mean Scottish father was in a bit of a quandary. His son wanted a dog and his daughter wanted a cat. Expensive items – and he felt that both would be a frivolous purchase. So he bought a cat and taught it to bark!

An Englishman was sent to work on the Isle of Skye for a month. On the first day it was overcast and it rained. On the second day it was overcast and it rained. The next day it rained and was overcast. On the fourth day it just rained. In fact it did the same on every other day of his stay. On his last day as he trudged to the bay to catch the ferry home he saw a small boy and asked him,

'Does the weather ever change here?'

'I don't know,' said the small boy. 'I'm only eight years old.'

'Oh come on, Jock,' said the Englishman as they discussed the merits of the home of the brave. 'Take away the majestic mountains, the beautiful glens and the many picturesque lochs and what have you got?'

'England!' smiled Jock.

Two musicians were discussing the merits of the bagpipes.

'Of course, you know the difference between a set of bagpipes and a lawnmower?' said one musician.

'I don't,' replied the other musician.

'Well,' answered the first musician, 'if someone borrows your lawnmower, you always ask for it back!'

How do you know when summer is coming to Scotland?

A Scotsman throws his Christmas tree away!

An Englishman got lost while walking in the wilds of the Scottish Highlands. He spent days upon days wandering around. He walked up mountains, down glens, through heather and swam many lochs, but he just couldn't find his way back to his wife and family. Finally one day he came across an old croft, where there sat an old kilted crofter.

'Oh thank goodness,' the Englishman cried. 'Can you help me? I've been lost for the last week and a half.'

The old crofter took a look at the bedraggled man and said, 'Oh aye, and will there be a wee reward for finding ye?'

'No,' said the Englishman.

'Och,' replied the crafty old crofter. 'Then I'm afraid ye are still lost!'

NEWSFLASH!
Sottish police arrested Jimmy Jimmy yesterday for breaking into a ten-pound note. Luckily for Mr Jimmy, he was let off, as it was his first offence!

Mary Ferguson went to see the local doctor regarding her husband's strange behaviour.

'Doctor, you've got to help me. There is something definitely wrong with my husband. He never listens to a word I say. What sort of complaint is that?'

'That's not a complaint,' grinned the doctor. 'That's a gift!'

Sadly Sandy MacDougall died and when he reached the Pearly Gates, St Peter boomed,

'And where do you come from?'

'Scotland,' said Sandy proudly.

'Oh, well you can go away then.'

'Why?' asked a puzzled Sandy.

'Well, if you think we're going to cook haggis for one person, you're sadly mistaken!'

In Italy, the Italian Mafia makes you an offer you can't refuse.

In Scotland, the Scottish Mafia makes you an offer you can't understand!

An Englishman went into a Scottish restaurant and was intrigued by an item on the menu. He called the waiter over and asked,

'So what is a Scottish breakfast?'

'That's a large bowl of porridge, a pound of oatcakes, a bottle of whisky and a large dog.'

'What's the large dog for?' asked a very puzzled Englishman.

'To eat the porridge and oatcakes!' replied the waiter.

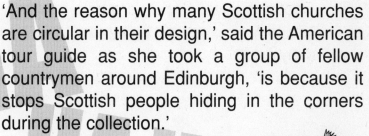

'And the reason why many Scottish churches are circular in their design,' said the American tour guide as she took a group of fellow countrymen around Edinburgh, 'is because it stops Scottish people hiding in the corners during the collection.'

Poor Mary McKarno was very ill. She lay on her deathbed with only the flicker of a candle to light up her weary and pale face. Her devoted husband, Tam, sat at her bedside.

'Tam, you need to go to work,' Mary said hoarsely.

'I know Mary,' sighed Tommy, 'but I don't want to leave you. Not tonight.'

Mary gathered up what was left of her dwindling strength and smiled.

'I'll be okay, Tam. You go.'

Tam gently kissed his wife on her forehead and stood up. At the bedroom door he stopped and looked back.

'Mary,' he whispered. 'If you do feel yourself slipping away, will you be sure to blow out the candle?'

How can you always tell you're at a Scottish wedding?

The confetti is on lengths of elastic!

Archie came rushing into the kitchen to talk to Maggie.

'Maggie, hen, great news. I've just found a fantastic job. It's good money, good prospects, great holidays and it's local with a fantastic pension plan,' he said excitedly.

'Och, that's wonderful,' smiled Maggie.

'There is one thing though,' said Archie. 'It's very long hours and the work is very hard and dirty.'

'Oh, that's no bad, if the money is good,' sympathised Maggie.

'Oh hen, I'm glad you see it that way,' smiled Archie. 'You start next week!'

Did you hear the one about Scotland's most unsuccessful switchboard operator?

She reverse-charged all the calls!

An old Scotsman was walking across a golf course when a stray golf ball hit him. Eventually the owner of the ball arrived and apologised profusely.

'Aye, that's no good enough,' growled the old Scotsman. 'I've got a weak heart. The shock could have killed me. Look, I demand £500 in compensation.'

'But I said "Fore",' said the golfer.

'Okay, done!' replied the old Scotsman.

At St Andrews a terrible golfer, having slashed his way round in 170, shouted at his Scottish caddie.

'You know what Jock, you must be the worst caddie in the world.'

Jock grinned and replied,

'Och nay sir, that would be just too much of a coincidence!'

Jamie was travelling on the London to Glasgow overnight train seated next to a Minister of the cloth. Feeling in need of a wee dram, Jamie took a bottle of whisky out of his jacket pocket. The Minister looked at him disapprovingly and said,

'Do you know? I'm nearly seventy-two and I've never tasted whisky in my life.'
Jamie smiled and poured himself a wee dram and said,

'Dinnae worry Reverend. There's no risk of you starting now!'

NEWSFLASH!
The Scottish Football team manager has picked his team to win the next World Cup... It's Brazil!

A man was driving through a tough Scottish town when his car got a puncture. He got out of the car, jacked it up and began to take the wheel off. While he was doing this a tough looking Scotsman walked up and casually lifted up the car's bonnet.

'What are you doing?' asked the surprised man.

'Och, it's only fair big man,' said the Scot. 'If you're having the wheels, I'm having the battery.'

Jamie and Jenny were rowing around a loch in a hired boat when the sky opened up and it rained and rained. Jamie and Jenny were getting drenched.

'Och Jenny,' moaned Jamie. 'We're getting soaked.'

'I know Jamie,' sniffed Jenny. 'I'll be glad when our hour is up so we can row back to the shore.'

A Scotsman went into a fancy seafood restaurant and ordered crab but wasn't too pleased when the dish was served.

'This crab has only got one claw,' he protested to the waiter.

'Ah, that's because he lost it in a fight with another crab, sir,' replied the waiter politely.

'Well,' said the Scotsman. 'He'd better be half price then!'

Jock and Tam were in an Art Gallery looking at a large abstract painting.

'What do you think?' asked Jock.

'Well Tam, I've often woken up in the morning with a hangover, but that's the first time I've seen a picture of one!'

Hamish runs into a Glasgow pub and shouts.

'Quick! Give me a pint of beer before the trouble starts.'

The landlord pours him a pint and Hamish knocks it back. No sooner has he finished than he says again,

'Quick! Give me another pint of beer before the trouble starts.'

Once again the landlord gives him another pint and asks as Hamish drains the glass,

'So what trouble is about to start?'

'Well,' says Hamish. 'I no have any money!'

Police have come up with a novel way of dispersing mobs of angry Scotsmen.

They rattle collection tins at them!

Want to know how to stop your expensive electric guitar from being stolen?

Put it in a bagpipe case!

Angus knew he had made a mistake, so he wrote a letter to his sweetheart:

Dearest Sweet Heather

I am so sorry about the things I said, I was drunk and not in control. I've had a lot of stress at work recently and I should have listened to you when you told me that drink never cures anything. It was drink talking when I broke off our engagement and it was drink that made me take up golf. Once again I am so sorry and would do anything, including giving up the drink, and even the golf, if you would just let me back into your life again. I love you so much and would like to spend the rest of my days with you in complete happiness.

Yours devotedly,

Angus

P.S. Congratulations on your recent big Lottery win.

'Mr MacTavish, may I have a word with you about your daughter?' asked the young man.

'Aye,' said Mr MacTavish.

'Well she has told me on many occasions that she loves me and that she can't possibly live without me and now she wants us to get married.'

Mr MacTavish smiled.

'Aye laddie and you want my permission to marry her?'

'Och no,' said the young lad. 'I want you to tell her to leave me alone!'

Maggie and Rhona were chatting over a cup of tea and some shortbread.

'So how's your daughter liking married life?' said Rhona.

'Oh fine,' answered Maggie. 'She lives in a big house, got two cars, a villa in Spain and all the jewellery she can eat. Only one problem though.'

'What's that?' asked Rhona.

'She cannae stand her husband.'

'Aye,' said Rhona. 'There's always something to spoil it!'

During the last war the Luftwaffe were venting their spleen on Glasgow. Maggie and Archie were in bed when the siren went off. Archie jumped out of bed and headed for the air raid shelter at the bottom of the garden. He had got to the foot of the stairs when he noticed that Maggie wasn't behind him.

'Maggie,' he called. 'Come on hen, what are you doing?'

'I'm looking for me false teeth,' Maggie called back.

'Leave them hen,' called Archie. 'They're dropping bombs – not sandwiches!'

Did you hear the one about the Scotsman who took his wife in for some plastic surgery?

He had her credit cards removed!

'I'm getting a wee bit worried,' Shona said to her friend as they drank a couple of cups of tea in their local tearoom, 'The Tartan Custard.'

'What is it Shona?'

'I keep seeing haggises. I saw one this morning at the foot of my bed. There was one in the bathroom and when I went downstairs there was one in the kitchen sink. There were a couple in the street and a load on the bus coming here and one standing outside this tearoom waiting for a taxi. It seems everywhere I go today, I keep seeing haggises.'

'Shona,' said her worried friend. 'Have you no seen a doctor?'

'No,' said Shona. 'Just haggises.'

Did you hear the one about the thrifty Scottish dad?

He used to tell his little son that the gas meter was a piggy bank!

Hamish was walking home from the pub one night when a nasty looking mugger jumped out in front of him.

'Okay Big Man,' snarled the mugger. 'Yer money or yer life!'

Hamish pondered a moment, then said,

'You'll have to take me life – me money's in the bank!'

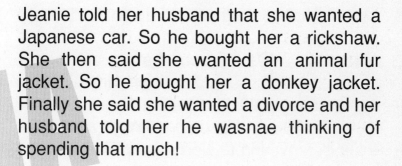

Jeanie told her husband that she wanted a Japanese car. So he bought her a rickshaw. She then said she wanted an animal fur jacket. So he bought her a donkey jacket. Finally she said she wanted a divorce and her husband told her he wasnae thinking of spending that much!

Cameron ran into his doctor and said,

'Doc help me, I think I'm going mad?'

'What's the problem?' asked the doctor as he practised his scribbling.

'Well yesterday I was walking down the road and a Mickey Mouse toy fell from the sky onto my head. Then in the evening when I was coming home from the pub a rubber Donald Duck fell from the sky and hit me on the head as well. Then this morning as I was putting the rubbish out, an inflatable Goofy fell from the sky and hit me on the head again. And to cap it all when I was coming to see you a load of *Lion King* DVDs fell from the sky and nearly knocked me out. Doctor is there anything you can do to stop this happening?'

'No,' said the doctor. 'Anyway I don't think it's anything to worry about.'

'Why?' asked a puzzled and sore-headed Cameron.

'Because it Disney matter!'

A Scotsman was travelling by train from Glasgow to London and was handing over his money for his ticket, when the man in the ticket booth said,

'By the way, don't forget – change at Crewe.'

The Scotsman looked at him and snarled,

'Aye, I'll have none of that laddie, I'll have my change now if you don't mind.'

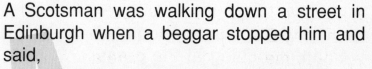

A Scotsman was walking down a street in Edinburgh when a beggar stopped him and said,

'Pound for a cup of tea, please Sir.'

The Scot looked at the beggar and replied,

'Right okay, but let's see the cup of tea first.'

So how do you get bagpipe players to play in unison?

Hide their bagpipes and give them toys!

A Scotsman was out walking in the countryside when he saw an old tramp in a field eating grass.

'What you doing man?' he asked.

'Och sir, I've no home and no money, this grass is all I can afford to eat.'

The Scotsman felt very sorry for the old tramp and invited him to his home.

'That's very kind of you sir,' said the tramp. 'But do you see that lassie over by the tree eating grass?'

The Scotsman looked and sure enough there was an equally bedraggled woman munching at the grass.

'Well,' continued the tramp. 'That is my sweet wife. Can she come with me?'

'Of course she can,' said the Scotsman.

The Scotsman and the tramp and his wife were about to leave when the tramp said,

'Excuse me sir, but do you see those two wee bairns over by that bush eating the grass?'

The Scotsman looked again.

'Yes I can,' he said.

'They are our wee bairns and well,

could they come with us too?' the tramp asked.

'Och, now steady on,' said the Scotsman. 'How big do you think my garden is?'

Managing to swim to the safety of a desert island Andrew McAndrew and Archie McArchie sat on the beach and watched the ship they were on only moments ago sink to the bottom of the ocean.

'Och well, it could have been worse,' said Archie.

'How?' asked Andrew.

'We could have bought return tickets,' smiled Archie.

Two Scottish photographers were chatting about their day over a pint and whisky chaser.

'I was over in the Gorbals this morning,' said the first photographer, 'when I saw this young homeless lass. She looked really tired and dishevelled and told me that she hadn't eaten for a week and hadn't anywhere to live and was taking what anyone could give her.'

'Och the poor wee lassie,' said the second photographer. 'So what did you give her?'

'Well the light wasnae too bad, so I gave her f-16 at 1/100.'

Did you hear about the Scottish mother who found a bottle of cough mixture?

She sent her children out to play in the rain in their pyjamas!

Cameron and Jeanie had just got married and were on their honeymoon in the Caribbean. After a relaxing day on the beach they were returning to their hotel room when a beautiful young girl came up to Cameron, kissed him and said,

'Hello darling,' and then walked away.

Once Cameron and Jeanie got to their room, Jeanie questioned him in no uncertain terms.

'And just *who* was that girl who just kissed you?'

'Och don't start hen,' sighed Cameron. 'I'm going to have enough trouble trying to explain who *you* are to *her!*'

How can you be sure that a Scotsman is dead?

Easy. Take him to his local pub during Happy Hour and go through his pockets. If he doesn't move...he's dead!

The McDougals were having a family picnic on the banks of Loch Ness when their youngest daughter came running up to them.

'Mummy, Daddy!' she screamed. 'I've just see the Loch Ness Monster.'

'Where?' asked the Dad.

'Not far from the bank,' the daughter sobbed. 'Oh Daddy it was horrible. It was all wrinkly and scaly with a really scary and ugly face.'

The dad looked out into the Loch and saw what his daughter had seen.

'Quick hen,' he said to his wife. 'Get a towel. Your mother has gone skinny dipping again.'

'I see a Scotsman has bought the local petrol station,' said one villager to another.

'How do you know he's Scottish?' asked the other villager.

'All the "Free Air" signs have been taken down.'

Archie and Andrew had gone deep-sea fishing for the day, but a storm had blown up and capsized their boat. Hanging on to the upturned hull as they were being swept out to sea, Archie said,

'Och Andrew, it's turned out to be a rotten day, hasn't it?'

'Aye,' said Andrew. 'It's a good job we didn't go mountain climbing today.'

Did you hear the one about the silly Scottish inventor?

He crossed a chicken with a cement mixer and got a bricklayer!

It's a well-known fact that on the Isle of Skye it only rains twice a year.

October to May, and June to September!

Maggie, a proud and bonny Scottish lass, was listening to two Englishwomen discussing their future holiday.

'I say, I think I'm going to Portugal, the Algarve. I've got a friend there who owns a lovely little villa on the beach,' said the first woman.

'Darling, you don't want to go there,' the second woman sneered. 'It's full of Scottish people.'

'Oh dear,' said the first woman. 'So where are you going?'

'I'm cruising the Med dear.'

'On which boat?' asked her friend

'*The Gleneagle* I think,' replied the woman.

'Oh no, not *The Gleneagle*!' shrieked her friend. 'I went on that last year and it was full of Scottish people.'

'Oh dear,' repeated the first friend. 'So where shall we go?'

'Why don't you go home?' interrupted Maggie. 'There's no any Scots there!'

A Scottish dad and his young son walked past a bike shop, which had in the window a fantastic looking, though expensive, Mountain Bike.

'See that bike, Sonny?' said the dad to his excited son. 'I want you to keep your eye on it.'

'Wow!' replied the young boy full of expectation. 'I will.'

'Good, because yer no be getting your backside on it!'

Hector was amazed when he found out that his friend, Hamish, had spent £300 on a weekend course about reincarnation.

'£300!' said Hector. 'What ever made you part with that much money?'
Hamish sighed and replied,

'Och, well, you only live once!'

A woman ran into a Scottish chemist's shop crying her eyes out.

'Do you realise what you've done?' she sobbed to the chemist.

'No?' replied the puzzled chemist.

'Instead of giving my husband cough mixture, you gave him rat poison.'
The chemist was shocked, 'Och, I'm awful sorry, hen.'

'What shall I do?' pleaded the wife.
The chemist thought and then said,
'Well you can give me the extra two pound you owe me!'

Jock was fuming at his wife.

'You daft woman. Why on earth did you lock the wee dog in the boot of the car? That's got to be the most stupid thing you've ever done.'

'Oh I don't know,' said his wife sheepishly. 'Wait until I tell you what I've done with the car keys!'

'What's the matter Jock?' asked Willie when he saw his pal looking very disheartened.

'Och, Willie. It's me kilt.'

'What's wrong with it?' asked Willie.

'Well I've just washed it and now I can't do a fling with it!'

'I cannae come down the pub tonight,' Jimmy told his pal who had rung with an invitation. 'It's the wife. She's doing bird impressions.'

'What do you mean?' asked his puzzled pal.

Jimmy sighed and said,

'She's watching me like a hawk!'

Jock and Tam were walking by the canal when they saw a man struggling in the water.

'Look over there Tam. Isn't that Hughie McBlewie, the bagpipe player?'
Tam looked.

'Aye it is, and he looks like he's drowning. Quick – we should throw him something.'

'What shall we throw him?' asked Jock.

'Well you can start with his bagpipes!'

'Now Mr McVitie, you have got to stop the deep-fried pizzas,' said the doctor. 'You have very high blood pressure.'

'How high?' asked McVitie.

'Well, put it this way,' replied the doctor, 'if you didn't have skin, you'd be a fountain!'

Did you hear the one about the Scotsman who hated gardening?

He concreted his windowbox!

It was a sad day when the Englishman, the Irishman and the Scotsman heard that the world was coming to an end. The Englishman went out and got very drunk. The Irishman went to confession to confess all his sins. The Scotsman organised a closing down sale!

'You're looking very pleased with yourself this morning Hector. Why's that?' said Hamish.

'Well you know how us Scots have a reputation of being tight and ungenerous?'

'Aye,' replied Hamish.

'Well last night I threw caution to the wind and went all extravagant.'

'You never,' said a shocked Hamish. 'What did you do?'

'I gave my canary an extra seed for his tea!'

'I had a group of bagpipe players standing on my doorstep the other day,' said Big May as she and Wee Mary were enjoying a cup of tea and some Dundee cake in a tearoom.

'What? With all their bagpipes?' asked Wee Mary.

'No, they didn't have any bagpipes with them,' replied Big May.

'Well how did you know they were bagpipe players?'

'No one knew when to come in!' said Big May.

Young Tam O'Shanter ran in to his father and proudly announced,

'Dad, I ran all the way home behind the bus and saved fifty pence.'
His Dad, being an even more thrifty Scot, replied,

'Och ye silly wee lad. Why dinnae ye run home behind a taxi and save yourself ten pounds?'

Two entertainers were having a meal in a restaurant. One was English and the other was Scottish. When the bill came the Scotsman said,

'I'll pay for that.'

The next day in the local paper a headline read:

'English ventriloquist killed in local restaurant.'

A skint Scotsman walked into a barber's shop and asked,

'How much for a haircut?'

'Five pounds,' answered the barber.

'And how much is it for a shave?'

'Three pounds,' replied the barber.

The Scotsman thought for a while and then said,

'Okay, shave my head.'

Big Hughie is pulled over by the police after they see his car weaving down the road.

'Will you blow into this breathalyser tube, please Sir,' asked PC Wurrald.

'Sorry, officer, I cannae do that,' said Big Hughie. 'You see I'm an asthmatic and if I blow into that wee tube, I could have a really bad asthma attack.'

PC Wurrald was understanding and said,

'Okay, we won't do that, but you'll have to come down to the station and give a sample of blood.'

Big Hughie sighed.

'Och I cannae do that either. I am a haemophiliac. If I do that, I'll bleed to death.'

'Then we need a urine sample.'

'Och I'm really sorry Officer,' apologised Big Hughie. 'I cannae do that either. You see I am also a diabetic. If I give you a wee wee-wee, I'll get really low blood sugar.'

PC Wurrald was losing his patience.

'All right then, I want you to get out of your car and walk down this white line.'

'Nope, cannae do that either,' smiled Big Hughie.

'Why ever not?' snapped the policeman.

'I'm drunk!' beamed Big Hughie.

It's not that well known that the bagpipes are an invention of the Irish. They sold the instrument to the Scots as a joke, and the Scots still haven't seen the joke yet!

Penny McPincher was so broke and penniless that she had to do something she found disgraceful.

She had to draw some money out of her bank account!

What's the difference between the Scottish World Cup winners and the Loch Ness Monster?

More people have seen the Loch Ness Monster!

Willie Swipeit was caught trying to steal a watch from an exclusive jewellery shop in Edinburgh.

'Och I know you no want any trouble,' Willie said to the manager who had caught him. 'So why don't I just pay you for this watch and we'll forget about the whole thing.'
The manager agreed and told Willie that the watch would cost him £700.

'£700!' gasped Willie. 'I wasnae thinking about spending that much. Can you show me something a little less expensive?'

A Scottish window cleaner by the name of Ken McWindow slipped from his ladder and fell to the ground breaking his ankle. A passerby ran to his rescue and seeing his predicament called to other onlookers,

'Quick, get this man a glass of water, while I phone for an ambulance.'
The man was about to call when Ken grabbed his arm and said,

'Och, big man, how far does a laddie have to fall to get a wee dram?'

An English tourist went into a Scottish gift shop, bought a tiny box of highland toffees and handed over a twenty-pound note and left the shop without waiting for his change. The Scottish shopkeeper was naturally concerned, and tried to attract the Englishman's attention by banging frantically on his shop window with a feather!

NEWSFLASH!
It has been reported that the game of golf was not invented in Scotland as everyone thinks. Mind you it does stand to reason. What Scotsman would be silly enough to invent a game where it is possible to lose a ball?

What do you call a Scottish bank-robber?

Rab D. Bank!

Andrew was a reporter on the little known newspaper *The Pitlochry Prattle* and was looking for a story when he came across a road accident. Although he couldn't see what had happened because of the large crowd of people that had gathered, he sensed it was quite a serious one. He needed to get to see what was going on, and report it, so he had an idea.

'Let me through, let me through!' he shouted as he hustled his way through the crowd. 'I'm the victim's son.'
The crowd parted and when he got to the front he found a dead donkey lying in front of a lorry!

A Scotsman was about to get on a bus with his pet crocodile.

'Hey, you cannae bring that thing on here! What are you doing man? You should take it to Edinburgh Zoo!' exclaimed the driver.

'I did!' said the Scotsman, 'and today I'm taking him to the park.'

Two Scotsmen went into a pub and ordered two pints of heavy and two whisky chasers, which they silently downed in one. Then they ordered the same again and silently drank them down very quickly. Then they ordered another round, drank that in silence, ordered another round and silently drank that too. They ordered the fifth round and just before they were about to drink it, one of the Scotsmen said,

'Cheers!'

The other Scotsman turned round and said,

'Look Tam, did we come here for a drink or to talk all night?'

It's not true that all Scotsmen are tight with their money. One Scotsman once offered £50,000 to the first person who could swim the Atlantic!

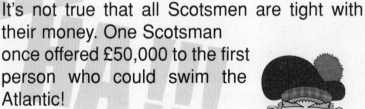

Old Jock went into his local church to have a chat with his Minister about something that was worrying him.

'What is it Jock?' asked the Minister.

'During the war I hid a deserter in my attic. He was only a young wee laddie and I felt sorry for him.'

'Well, that's not a sin, in fact it's quite a courageous thing to do in the circumstances,' said the Minister.

'I'm afraid I also charged him five pounds a week for hiding there.'

'Well that's not something to be proud of, but what you did was a brave and Christian thing on your part.'

'Aye,' replied Old Jock, still looking worried.

'Jock are you okay? It was a long time ago and I think God will have forgiven you by now.'

'Thank you,' smiled Old Jock. He turned to leave, then stopped.

'Just one more thing.'

'What is it?' the Minister asked.

'Do you think I should tell him the war is over?'

McGregor owned a family run shop in Glasgow, but now he was nearing the end of his life. As he lay in his bed, his eyes closed and with his family around him he whispered,

'Is Jeanie here?'

'Aye Daddy,' wept Jeanie. 'I'm here.'

'Is Rory here?'

Rory moved to his father's bedside.

'Aye Dad, I'm right here.'

'And is my dear wife here?'

McGregor's wife was beside herself but managed a brave smile.

'Aye darling, I'm here.'

Suddenly McGregor opened his eyes, sat up and hollered,

'Then *who* is looking after the shop?'

Did you hear the one about the silly Scottish oilrig worker?

He used to throw bread to the helicopters!

Rory McLion loved frying things. In fact everything he ate, he fried: not just bacon and eggs, but peas and beans. Even puddings, rice puddings, jelly, trifle, cakes, Mars bars, crisps: you name it, he fried it. So great was this obsession with frying, he even started to fry the newspaper, his shoes, his clothes and even his bicycle. Obviously his family were getting very worried. They thought he was just frittering his life away!

A Scotsman was speaking to an Englishman.

'Och, do you know. All I want to do is buy the woman I love a wee croft up on the banks of Loch Lomond, where we can always be together.'

'But you won't because you're Scottish and you can't bear to part with the money?' said the Englishman.

'No, it's not that,' replied the Scotsman.

'Why won't you do it then?' asked the Englishman.

'My wife won't let me,' sighed the Scotsman.

Willie had downed 12 pints of heavy too many and was hanging onto a lamppost next to a bus stop when a policeman appeared.

'Come on laddie, you've been standing here for ages. Time to go home.'

'No, I'm okay,' burped Willie. 'You see it's a well-known fact that the world goes round every 24 hours, so I'm just waiting here for my house to come by. It won't be long because that's my next door neighbour waiting at the bus stop.'

Sandy went into a Scottish restaurant and saw on the menu Chicken Tarka. He called the waiter over and said,

'I think you have got a wee spelling mistake in your menu. You've got Chicken Tarka. Should that be Chicken Tikka?'

'Oh no Sir,' says the waiter. 'It's correct. It's like Chicken Tikka, but a little 'otter!'

'Och Tam, I have a wee problem,' said Angus McCoatup when he met up with his old pal.

'What's the problem?' asked Tam.

'Well I've got a big house in the Highlands, a flat in the middle of Edinburgh, a villa in Portugal, an apartment in Miami and an Island in the Pacific and I've just bought my third Ferrari.'

'Wow!' gasped Tam. 'How can all that be a problem?'

'I only earn two hundred pounds a week,' sighed Angus.

McTavish was downing pints as fast as the barman could pull them.

'Hey big man!' said the barman. 'Slow down.'

'I can't,' replied McTavish. 'Not since that terrible accident I had one night in a bar in Fife.'

'What terrible accident?' asked the curious barman.

'Och it was terrible,' replied McTavish. 'I knocked my glass over with my elbow.'

A Scotsman in a kilt walks into a fancy restaurant carrying a bulging plastic bag under his arm and the Maître d' asks,

'What's in the bag?'

'Eight pounds of haggis,' the Scotsman replies.

'Oh thank goodness for that,' sighed the Maître d'. 'For a minute, I thought it was bagpipes!'

Old Jock was going deaf, but being mean he didn't want to part with any money to buy a hearing aid. So being a canny Scot, he came up with the perfect solution. He borrowed a piece of flex from his neighbour, put one end around his ear and another in his top pocket. It didn't help him hear better, but people did speak to him with raised voices.

Hughie and Louise were lovers and together they strolled arm in arm along the bonny, bonny banks of Loch Lomond.

'Oh look Hughie,' Louise sighed. 'Look at those wee birds a-skimming and a-swooping across the water, flapping their wings a hundred times a minute!'

'Aye, 'tis a wonderful sight,' Hughie answered softly.

'And look,' continued Louise. 'Do you see that they have their beaks together?'

'Aye hen, I do,' smiled Hughie.

'Oh Hughie,' swooned Louise. 'Come on. Let's do that.'

'Och hen, we can try, but I cannae flap my arms that fast,' sighed Hughie.

Maggie and Rhona were chatting over the garden fence.

'I see you've had people round for tea,' said Rhona.

'How did you know?' asked Maggie.

'I saw the tea bags on your washing line,' replied Rhona.

An old Scotswoman went into her local church-run fish and chip shop called 'In Cod We Trust' and spoke to the assistant behind the counter.

'Sonny, I want a small cod, a small portion of chips, a cheap battered sausage and a wee sprinkling of salt and vinegar.'

'Certainly madam,' said the assistant. 'Anything else?'

'Och aye,' the old Scotswoman replied. 'Could you wrap it all up in today's newspaper?'

'Do you know that the police now have a machine that can tell if you're telling a lie?' said Jimmy as he and Tam were having a drink in their local bar 'The Closed Wallet'. 'Have you seen one?'

'Seen one?' sighed Jimmy. 'I married one.'

A Scottish car salesman in Falkirk was showing a potential buyer around a new car.

'It has all the basic safety features. ABS braking, twin airbags, side impact bars,' said the salesman. 'It also has a Radio, CD and DVD player and Satellite Navigation. A very special feature on this car is the quiet Scottish horn.'

'A Scottish horn?' asked the potential buyer. 'What does that do?'

'It hoots, man!' replied the salesman.

An Irishman was visiting some old graveyards in Aberdeenshire when he came across a headstone that read:

"Here lies a generous man, a devoted father, and a great scholar."

'Bejabers!' exclaimed the Irishman. 'Only the Scots would bury three men in one grave.'

Two burglars broke into a house in Scotland in search of some money. They were caught by the owner, Big Bad Bruce, but after a struggle managed to escape with some money and lots of bruises.

'That's wasnae too bad,' said one of the burglars later. 'We came out with twenty pound.'

'Aye,' said the other burglar, 'but we had fifty pounds on us when we broke in.'

'Hector, is it no true, that you are a great believer in free speech?' asked Hamish as he sat in his friend's living room.

'Aye, that's very true,' said Hector proudly.

'Oh good,' replied Hamish. 'Then you'll no mind if I use your phone?'

A man went into an Edinburgh music shop and approached the assistant.

'I'd like that red saxophone and that white accordion please.'

The assistant sighed and said,

'You're a bagpipe player aren't you?'

'How did you know?' the man said with a hint of surprise in his voice.

'Because it's a well known fact that bagpipe players know nothing about music.'

'How dare you!' exclaimed the man. 'I'll have you know I'm an accomplished musician and just because I play the bagpipes that does not make me musically stupid. So are you going to sell me that red saxophone and white accordion, or not?'

The assistant took a beep breath.

'Well, the fire extinguisher I can do a deal on, but the radiator stays where it is.'

Penny McPincher was so tight that she changed her name to OVO5 JYM just so she could have her own personalised numberplate.

A golfer was having a particularly bad game, spending more time in the rough and off course than he did on the fairways. Obviously he was getting frustrated and angry and wasn't too pleased with his old Scottish caddie.

'Why do you keep looking at your watch?' he snapped.

'It's no a watch,' said the caddie. 'It's a compass!'

'So where are you from?' The Scotsman asked the Englishman after they had chatted for while in a Glasgow bar.

'I'm from the finest country in the world,' the Englishman said.

'Really?' replied the Scotsman. 'Well, that's the strangest Scottish accent I've ever heard!'

An Englishman and a Scotsman were playing a round of golf together on the hallowed course of St Andrews. After the first hole the Englishman asked,

'So how many did you take on that hole?'

'Five,' said the Scot.

'Oh well done,' smiled the Englishman. 'I took four, so that makes it my hole.'

On the second hole the Englishman asked again,

'So how many do you take on that hole?'

'Seven,' said the Scot.

'Hard luck,' said the Englishman. 'I took six, so that makes it my hole again.'

On the third hole the Englishman once again asked the question, but this time the Scotsman said,

'Aye, hang about laddie, this time it's my turn to ask first.'

Amongst the Lost and Found pages of the *Glasgow Herald* was an item that read:

'Lost: £10 note. Has sentimental value!'

Old Jock went to see his private doctor.

'Och doctor, it's me memory. I think it's going. I can barely remember a thing. What do you advise?'

The Scottish doctor thought for a while and then said,

'Well you can pay me in advance for a start.'

George, Patrick and Andrew were each left £10,000 by a very rich friend on the condition that when he passed away each of them would put £100 in his coffin just in case he needed the money to spend in heaven. When the rich man died, the three men stood around the open coffin and George, the Englishman put in his £100 pounds. Then Patrick, the Irishman, placed his £100 in the coffin. It was now the turn of Andrew, the Scotsman. He thought for a while then took the £200 pounds out of the coffin and put in a cheque for £300!

57

An English golfer and his Scottish caddie were just returning from the last hole of a disastrous round of golf, and as they headed for the 19th hole, they walked past a lake and the golfer said,

'Do you know what Jock? I'm so depressed with the way I played today, I've a good mind to jump in that lake and drown myself.'

'I doubt if you could keep your head down long enough, Sir,' replied the caddie!

Poor old Hughie McScrewy was dying in hospital so as a final request he asked the nurse if a bagpiper could come into the ward and play a few tunes to see him on his way. The nurse agreed and the piper arrived and duly played. Amazingly Hughie recovered and got better, but everyone else in the ward died.

'Archie, why don't you play golf with Billy any more?' asked Archie's wife one morning.

'Well,' began Archie, 'would you play with anyone who cheats by moving their ball when no one is looking, lies about the number of strokes they took and never buys a round after the game?'

'Of course not,' said Archie's wife.

'Neither would Billy,' replied Archie.

Owing to the fact that she said he was spending too much time down the pub, Jock took his wife Jessie to his local bar one night and bought a pint for himself and another pint for his wife. Jessie took a sip of her pint and was disgusted.

'Urgh! This is awful, how do you drink this stuff every night?'

'There you go hen,' said Jock. 'And you thought I came here to enjoy myself?'

Cameron has just worked his first day on the oil-rig and in the evening he goes to the crew's bar area. The place is dead. No pool table, no dartboard, nothing – apart from a barman, a very pretty barmaid, and a gorilla sitting in the corner.

'What do you do for fun around here, pal?' Cameron asked the barman.

'I'll show you laddie,' said the barman. The barman picks up a cricket bat and goes over to the corner of the bar where a gorilla is sitting and hits him over the head with it. The gorilla goes crazy. It jumps all over that place, smashing tables and glasses and finally leaps over the bar and gives the pretty barmaid a kiss.

'Och that's amazing,' said Cameron. 'Especially when he kisses the barmaid.'

'Right, laddie. Do you want a go?' asked the barman slapping the cricket bat.

'Aye, okay,' said Cameron. 'But don't hit me as hard with the bat.'

'I've been reading how bad buns and cakes are for you,' Big May said to her friend Wee Mary in the tearoom. 'So I've given up.'
Wee Mary was shocked.

'I don't believe it May, you've actually given up buns and cakes?'

'Och no,' Big May smiled. 'I've given up reading.'

Jeanie went into a tough Scottish fish and chip shop called 'The Bruised and Battered Cod' and asked for some fish and chips.

'Certainly hen,' said the man behind the counter. 'The fish won't be long.'

'Well, give me plenty of chips then,' replied Jeanie.

Farmer McDonald found the perfect way to stop his rooster crowing early on a Monday morning. He ate him for Sunday dinner!

The Judge looked sternly at Stewart McPudding and said,

'Mr McPudding. You admit breaking into a dress shop on the night in question?'

'Aye, your honour,' said McPudding with his head hung low. 'But my wife made me do it.'

'And why was that?' asked the Judge.

'Because she wanted a new dress and I cannae afford to buy her one.'
The judge looked at his notes.

'That's as may be Mr McPudding, but it says here that you broke into the same dress shop twice in the same night. Once again I have to ask why?'
McPudding looked up and sighed,

'Because your honour, the wife dinnae like the colour, so I had to go back and exchange it.'

The Scots have invented a new watch. It doesn't need batteries or winding up and it has no face and no hands. How do you tell the time? Ask someone!

Did you hear about the Scottish boy who ate all the decorations off a Christmas tree?

He's OK now, but he was rushed to hospital with Tinselitus!

Hamish and Hector were having a drink around Hamish's house when they saw Tam walking up the path.

'Och, look out here comes the Exorcist,' said Hector.

'Why do you call him that?' asked Hamish.

'Because,' replied Hector, 'whenever he comes round my house, all the spirits disappear.'

An American tourist walked into a tough Glasgow pub and was impressed by what he saw.

'Gee, this is great,' he said to the barman. 'A real authentic Scottish pub. You've even got sawdust on the floor.'

'Och that isnae sawdust,' grinned the barman. 'That's last night's furniture!'

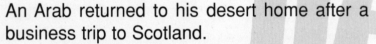

An Arab returned to his desert home after a business trip to Scotland.

'How was it?' asked his friend Mustafa.

'It was wonderful. The Scottish business folk are so friendly and generous.'

'And what about the Scottish salesmen?'

'Ah, they impressed me the most,' the Arab said as he strapped on his skis.

A Scotsman wrote in his diary:

'I am a very good man of Scottish blood. I no smoke, drink or gamble. I no stay out late in night-clubs or go to lap dancing clubs. I am faithful to my wife and have never strayed when enticed by the pleasures of female flesh. I go to bed early and wake at first light. I work for a full day and exercise hard and often. Obviously this will all change when I get out of prison.'

Willie Buildit was very proud of the house he had built on a very low budget and was showing a friend around the premises. All the rooms were very impressive, apart from one room next to the bathroom.

'Willie,' asked his friend, 'this room has no roof. Could you no afford it?'

'Och no,' smiled Willie. 'That's the shower.'

Wee Rab was walking through customs at Edinburgh airport with a big bottle under his arm. One of the customs officials stopped him and asked,

'What's in the bottle, laddie?'

'It's full of holy water from my trip to Lourdes,' replied Wee Rab, but the customs officer was still suspicious. So suspicious in fact that he took the bottle from Wee Rab, unscrewed the lid and took a swig of its contents.

'This isnae Holy Water,' he spluttered. 'This is pure whisky!'

'Whisky?' shouted Wee Rab. 'It's another miracle!'

A Scotsman was explaining the rules of golf to his wife.

'Och I see,' said his wife. 'So the less times I hit the ball the better I am?'

'That's right hen,' said the Scotsman.

His wife thought for a while and then asked,

'So why hit the ball at all?'

'I'd like a job,' said McShifty to the assistant behind the counter in the job centre.

'I think I might have the very thing for you,' said the assistant. 'A new whisky distillery has just opened and is looking for someone to be a whisky taster. Your working hours would be from 10am until 2pm with two hours for lunch. You will be expected to drink as much whisky as you can and you will be paid £1000 a week, with a pension and 12 weeks holiday. Oh, and just one more thing, this distillery is quite unusual as it run by part-time supermodels.'

'You're joking!' said the open-mouthed McShifty.

'Well you started it!' replied the assistant.

Jock got a job in a local distillery as a whisky taster for £50 a week.

It was all he could afford to pay them!

A Scotsman was on holiday in the wilds of Canada when one morning he looked out of his hotel window and saw a huge beast wander past. Not knowing what it was, he rushed down to reception and pointed out the large animal to the receptionist.

'What is it?' asked the Scotsman.

'It's a moose, sir,' replied the receptionist.

'A moose?' said the Scotsman, staring in disbelief at the animal. 'If that's a moose, how big are your cats around here?'

A Scottish piper was so fed up with people telling how awful his bagpipes sounded that he decided to take his pipes into the woods and play to his heart's content. This he did until the trees got up and walked away!

An Irishman was staying in a terrible Scottish hotel when he rang room service.

'Room service,' said the voice on the other end of the phone. 'How can I help you?'

'I don't seem to have a towel in my bathroom,' replied the Irishman.

'Och I'm sorry,' said room service. 'I'll send it up to you as soon as the man in room number 7 has finished with it.'

At the Dundee Dundee cake competition, the judge was very impressed with Ol' Maggie's iced cake entry.

'This is delicious,' beamed the judge as he took one of many mouthfuls. 'I especially like this icing. Tell me, how did you manage to get such a lovely gloss on the icing?'

'Och that's easy,' smiled Ol' Maggie. 'I lick it a lot.'

McTavish the gamekeeper was given a Deerstalker hat for Christmas. He was particularly impressed with the earflaps that could be pulled down on cold and windy days to keep his ears warm. Unfortunately he had to stop wearing it when he was involved in a nasty accident. He was in a pub one lunchtime, with the earflaps down and he didn't hear someone offer to buy him a large whisky.

Frazer and Katie had been out on a walk during their first date. As they stood on Katie's doorstep and exchanged a chaste kiss, a slightly disappointed Katie said to Frazer,

'Now you be careful walking home, sweetheart. I would hate to hear that you've been mugged and been robbed of all the money you saved this evening.'

A Scotsman had enjoyed his meal in a fancy Edinburgh restaurant and was about to leave when he dropped a 10p piece. He called the waiter over.

'Excuse me, I've dropped a 10p piece. If you find it, I'd like it back. If you don't, you can have it as a tip.'

Did you hear the one about the Scotsman who deposited all his money in a bank?

He asked the bank manager when the visiting times were!

Wee old Maggie MacCardy asked the bus conductor,
'I say laddie. Does this bus stop at the river?'
'I hope so,' said the conductor. 'Otherwise there's going to be a big splash.'

Scott and Jock were having a discussion on the subject of whisky.

'So Jock,' asked Scott. 'What do ye think of the ol' Irish whiskey?'

'Och it's no bad,' replied Jock, 'especially if you run out of water to add to Scotch whisky!'

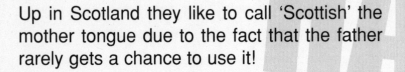

Up in Scotland they like to call 'Scottish' the mother tongue due to the fact that the father rarely gets a chance to use it!

Sandy met his local church minister in the golf club house.

'Tell me Reverend, do you think it wrong of me to play golf on a Sunday?'

The Minister thought for a moment, then said,

'The way you played Sandy, it's a sin any day of the week.'

There was knock on Ol' Maggie's door and when she opened there was a worried looking man on her doorstep.

'I'm really sorry,' he stammered. 'But I've just run over your dog and killed it.'

'Oh dear, that is a shame,' said Maggie.

'I am so sorry,' the man apologised. 'I'd like to replace it.'

'Fine,' smiled Ol' Maggie. 'How good are you at chasing postmen?'

Wee Jimmy ran into the living room and shouted,

'Dad, Dad, there's boiling water coming out of the radiator.'

'Aye, no panic,' said his Dad. 'But dinnae waste it – fetch the tea bags!'

Two tourists were climbing in the Cairngorms when after many hours they became hopelessly lost. Fred studied his map, consulted his compass, and even tried to work out their position according to the sun. Finally, he turned to his companion.

'George, you see that mountain over there?' he said pointing westward.

'Yes,' answered George.

'Well according to this map, we're standing on top of it!'

'Och, I had a terrible dream last night,' Hamish told Hector. 'I dreamt that I was on a desert island surrounded by three hundred beautiful, buxom, red-haired Scottish lassies in wee tartan mini-skirts. It was awful.'

'Why was that awful?' asked a puzzled Hector.

Hamish sighed,

'I was a lassie too!'

A tourist walked into a bar in Montrose and announced that he would give twenty pounds to anybody in the pub who was contented with life. One Scot, eager to make some money put his hand up and called,

'Hey big man, over here! I'm a contented man. A really, really contented man.'

'Then why do you want my twenty pounds?' answered the tourist.

A Scotsman went into his local newsagents one Sunday morning and noticed that the *Glasgow Weekly* was going up on Monday from 30 pence to 40 pence, so being a thrifty Scot and wanting to save money, he bought all the copies the shop had!

Tam was a complete atheist and was fishing in Loch Ness when the monster rose from the deep and tossed his boat high into the air. As Tam fell from the boat he could see that he was falling straight into the jaws of the beast.

'Oh my God!' he screamed. 'Help me!' Suddenly everything froze. Time had stood still. Then a huge booming voice was heard from beyond the clouds.

'I thought you didn't believe in Me!' a voice echoed around the loch.

'Och, come on, do us a favour!' shouted Tam. 'A couple of seconds ago I dinnae believe in the Loch Ness monster either.'

'Archie!' called Maggie one morning as he set off for work. 'Why are you taking my false teeth with you to the office?'

'To stop you eating between meals!' Archie called back.

An Irishman and a Scotsman met in a pub one evening and got chatting.

'You know that playing the bagpipes is like being a blindfolded javelin thrower?' said the Scotsman.

'What do you mean?' asked the Irishman.

'Well you don't have to be that good to get people's attention!'

Jock went into a barber in the tough part of Edinburgh.

'Morning sir,' growled the barber. 'Are you new to the area?'

'No,' replied Jock. 'I've been here before.'

The barber looked at Jock for a while and then said,

'No, I don't recognise your face.'

'Probably not,' replied Jock. 'It's healed up since I was here last.'

A student was staying in a very run down bed-sit and one day went to his Scottish landlord to complain.

'I don't like all the rats in my room,' the student moaned.

'That's no bother, laddie,' replied the landlord. 'You show me the ones you do like and I'll get rid of the rest for you!'

'Hey Hector,' said Hamish as they met in the supermarket haggis section one day. 'Did you read about the Scot who has invented an infallible way to stop Scotsmen getting seasick?'

'No I didn't,' said Hector.

'Apparently when you feel sick, you put a pound coin in your mouth and lean over the side of the ship and you daren't be sick.'

So what do you call a Scottish player in the first round of the World Cup?

The referee!

Macdonald was still mourning the loss of his beloved wife when the insurance man handed over the cheque for £75,000.

'Seventy-five thousand pounds,' Macdonald sighed. 'Seventy-five thousands, it's no much for a life of love, faith and companionship is it?'
He wiped away a tear and took a deep breath.

'You know I would gladly give a third of this back to have the wee wife back again.'

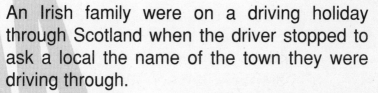

An Irish family were on a driving holiday through Scotland when the driver stopped to ask a local the name of the town they were driving through.

'It'll cost you a pound to tell you,' replied the local.

'Ah, that would make this Inverness,' said the driver and drove off.

Ol' Maggie lived on the third floor of a tenement block. One day she broke her leg and was told by her doctor not to climb any stairs. Months passed and soon the cast around her leg was removed.

'That seems to be mended now, Maggie,' the doctor told her.

'Oh that's great doctor,' said Ol' Maggie, relieved. 'Will I be able to climb the stairs again?'

'Of course,' replied the doctor.

'Och that's grand,' Maggie said. 'I'm so sick and tired of climbing up and down that drainpipe.'

An English tourist arrived at a small boarding house on the Isle of Skye and on entering noticed the words 'Tam Htab' written on the doormat.

'I guess that's the Gaelic for welcome,' he said.

'Och no,' said the hotel keeper. 'That's just the bath mat upside down.'

A very brave Irishman had seen the young Scottish lass drowning in the unforgiving waters of Loch Lomond and had dived in and pulled her to the bank, where, surrounded by onlookers, he had given artificial respiration. The lass's parents broke through the crowd just as their daughter began to recover and were obviously overjoyed.

'Och Archie,' the wife said to her husband. 'Give that brave, brave man ten pounds for saving our daughter's life.'

'But mum I was half dead!' spluttered the young lass.

'Och in that case,' said the wife, 'give him five pounds.'

It's a well-known fact that Scottish lassies are amongst the prettiest girls in the world, but one of them certainly wasn't. Aggie McHaggie went for a swim in Loch Ness and the monster gave itself up!

Hughie was always looking for ways to save wear and tear on his wallet by not opening it. One day he asked a bus conductor how much it would cost him to travel in to town.

'A pound,' answered the conductor.
Thinking this was a wee bit expensive he decide that he would run after the bus for a few stops.

'How much now?' asked Hughie when the bus stopped a few stops later.

'Still a pound,' replied the conductor.
The bus pulled away and Hughie ran behind it. Finally the bus stopped at another stop. An exhausted Hughie asked,

'How much now?'

'One pound twenty.'

'One pound twenty!' gasped Hughie. 'It was only a pound at the last stop.'

'I know,' said the conductor, 'but you're running in the wrong direction!'

Stewart McStewart was Scotland's top life insurance salesman. If he was having any hesitation from potential customers to signing up for life insurance he used to say,

'Now don't worry about it. Think it over and don't let me rush you. Look, why don't you sleep on it overnight and *if* you wake up in the morning give me a call!'

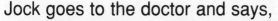

Jock goes to the doctor and says,

'Oh doctor, I swallowed ten pound worth of coins last month. Can ye get them out?'
The doctor looked puzzled.

'You swallowed the money last month, but only come to see me today?' he says. 'I don't understand, why have you left it so long?'

'I dinnae need the money then!' said Jock.

An alien walks into a crowded Scottish pub and says to the barman,

'Take me to your leader.'

The barman looks at the alien and says,

'You're not from round here are you?'

'No,' said the alien.

'Then I better explain. On earth, it costs you to see our leader.'

'It's okay,' said the alien. 'I have money.'

'Have you now?' grinned the barman. 'Enough to buy every one in this pub a bottle of best Scottish Malt whisky?'

'Of course!' smiled the alien. 'Then will you take me to your leader?'

'Oh aye,' said the barman as he began handing the bottles out. When he had finished he said to the alien,

'That'll be two hundred and fifty five pound and twenty-six pence.'

'Okay,' said the alien. 'And what's that in Zubars?'

A Scottish chemistry teacher confidently dropped a pound coin into a glass of acid. He then asked his students how he knew that the coin wouldn't dissolve.

'Because,' said one of the students, 'you would have never dropped it in there if it did!'

'I think you only married me Hughie McShewie, because my dad died and left me a million pounds!' screamed Mrs McShewie at her husband.

'Och hen,' said Hughie, 'I would have married you no matter who had died and left you a million pounds.'

Six drunken Scotsmen fall out of a pub. Which one drives them all home?

The one with the bagpipes!

Jocky and Jessie Cameron had just won 20 million pounds on the lottery and were obviously very pleased, especially Jessie who has spent all her working life as a cleaner.

'Aye, Jocky,' she sighed happily. 'After all those year a-scrubbing and a-cleaning, at last I can throw away that old scrubbing brush and broom.'

'That's right,' beamed Jocky. 'We can afford to buy you new ones now!'

Jeanie lay dying in her bed with her husband, Angus at her side.

'Angus,' she said with dying breath. 'Will you do me a wee favour?'

'Aye,' said Angus. 'What'll it be, hen?'

'On the day of my funeral I would like you to travel to the church in the same car as my mother. Will you do that for me Angus?'

'Well okay,' sighed Angus, 'but it'll completely spoil the day for me.'

A wee bonnie lassie ran to her mother and asked if she could have some money for a man who was crying outside.

'Och, what crying man?' asked her mother.

'The one that's crying, "Ice creams! Ice creams!"' grinned the lassie.

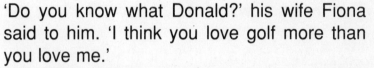

'Do you know what Donald?' his wife Fiona said to him. 'I think you love golf more than you love me.'

'Och Fiona, that may be true,' replied her husband, 'but always be thankful that I love you more than I love fishing.'

Mary arrived home from her weekly shop laden down with 6 cases of finest Scottish malt whisky and a Dundee cake.

'Good grief hen,' said her husband. 'What did you buy that cake for?'

Over the tannoy system, the passengers heard,

'Welcome to Scottish Air Budget flights. This is your captain Roger N Out speaking. We are about to take off so would you all please make sure your wallets are fastened.'

Two Irishmen went into a shabby looking bar in Glasgow.

'We'd like a pint of Guinness each,' said Patrick.

'And make sure mine's in a clean glass,' added Sean.

The Scottish barman went off to get the drinks and when he returned he asked,

'Okay, which one of you two jokers asked for the clean glass?'

Did you hear the one about the Scottish bride and groom who asked a relative to buy them a 50-piece dinner set for a wedding present?

He bought them a box of deluxe cocktail sticks!

Do you know it takes five bagpipe players to change a light bulb?

It's true. One to change the bulb and four to play a lament for the old one!

It's a well-known fact that Scottish football fans support two teams during the World Cup.

Scotland and whoever is playing against England!

An Englishman was walking past a Scottish pub when he saw a sign in the window, which read: 'Finest Scottish beer – 50p a pint'. Finding this hard to believe, he rushed into the pub and ordered his 50p pint. While he drank his pint, he noticed that the pub was full of Scots, which wasn't unusual considering he was in Scotland, but none of them were drinking, which was unusual. So he said to the barman,

'This beer is very cheap.'

'Och aye!' said the barman.

'It's very nice.'

'Och aye!' said the barman again.

'Why isn't anyone drinking it then?' said the Englishman.

'Och, they're waiting for happy hour!'

An English golfer was hacking lumps out of the St Andrews fairway as he tried for the umpteenth time to strike his ball.

'I say,' he said. 'The worms must think there is a earthquake going on!'

'I'll no worry about them,' replied his Scottish caddie. 'They'll probably be hiding under your ball for safety.'

Did you hear the one about the Scotsman who fell into the grave he had just dug?

He wasn't actually a gravedigger. He was just filling in for a friend!

NEWSFLASH!
The Scottish steeplechase was finally abandoned this afternoon because the horses couldn't get a decent grip on the church roof.

An Englishman and a Scotsman are walking down the road one day, when they see an old bottle in the gutter. The Englishman picks it up and tries to rub off the dirt, when suddenly a genie emerges in a plume of purple smoke.

'I'm the genie of the bottle and will give you each a wish!' booms the genie.
The Englishman thinks for a while then says, 'I'd like a wall built around England to protect that fair country from invasions and interlopers.'

'So be it,' says the genie. He waves his hand and suddenly there is a huge wall around England. The genie then turns to the Scotsman and asks what his wish would be.

'Can you tell me a bit more about this wall around England?' he asks.

'Well,' says the genie, 'it's 200 feet high and about 100 feet thick and runs along the English boundary. It's waterproof too.'

'Och, that's a grand job,' smiles the Scotsman.

'Thanks very much,' says the genie. 'Now what is your wish?'
The Scotsman looks at the Englishman and whispers to the genie,

'Could you fill it up with water?'

A dour Scottish laddie had met a bonny lass at the disco and when the dancing was coming to an end, the lass asked him,

'Okay, my place or yours?'

'Och, look,' moaned the laddie. 'If it's going to be a hassle, forget it.'

A theatre in Scotland was showing a murder mystery and Sandy had got a ticket but not a very good seat. Just before the play was about to start, Sandy went to the front row where another Scot was sitting.

'Excuse me, I was wondering if you would mind changing seats with me? I'll give you a very good tip.'

Like any true Scot the word 'Tip' was music to his ears and he got up and allowed Sandy to sit down.

'Is that okay?' asked the Scot.

'Och aye,' said Sandy.

'So what about my tip?'

'Och aye,' smiled Sandy. 'The butler did it!'

A Scotsman was sitting on a park bench crying his eyes out when a passer by stopped and asked,

'What's the matter?'

'I cannae believe it,' the Scotsman sobbed. 'The richest man in Scotland has just died.'

'Oh I'm sorry,' said the passer by. 'Were you related?'

'No!' cried the Scotsman even louder.

A highland hunter had caught a particularly fine specimen of a duck and took it to his local taxidermist to get stuffed and mounted. The hunter returned a few days later but his duck was nowhere to be seen.

'I'm so sorry,' apologised the taxidermist. 'I cannae stuff the duck.'

'Why's that?' asked the hunter.

'It's got a quack in it!'

Robbie was on holiday in London and was on the phone to his mum.

'I tell you something, mum,' he said, 'they're not very friendly down here, especially in the hotel I'm staying at. Every morning at about 4 o'clock, people bang on my bedroom door, on the walls, on the floor and the ceiling. It's so noisy I can hardly hear myself playing the bagpipes!'

Maggie's mother had died and she and her husband, Archie, were discussing how the old girl should exit the world.

'What do you think, Archie,' asked Maggie. 'Should we have her embalmed, cremated or buried?'

'All three,' Archie replied, thinking about his ex mother-in-law. 'We'd best take no chances!'

At the Battle of Bannockburn the English Army led by Edward the Second lay siege to Stirling Castle where King Robert the Bruce held strong. During the height of the battle a lone piper played on his bagpipes with all his might. The English attacked with spears, swords and arrows. Scotsmen fell by the tens and still the piper played on and the English kept coming. Scotsmen fell by the twenties and still the piper played on and the English kept coming. Scotsmen fell by the fifties and still the pipe played on and the English kept coming. Then in desperation King Robert the Bruce called out to the piper and said,

'For heaven's sake Hughie, can ye no play something they like?'

Two Scottish mothers were enjoying a cup of tea and a baked tatty at their local tearoom.

'What do you think your son will be when he passes his exams?' asked one.

'About 42,' sighed her friend.

Archie and Andrew had gone on a hunting trip to Canada and one night as they lay in their tent they were both disturbed by a wolf howl.

'I bet you twenty pounds you can't go out and kill that wolf,' Archie challenged Andrew.

Andrew took up Archie's challenge and about ten minutes later came back with the dead carcass of a wolf. Archie reluctantly handed over the twenty pound and they settled down for the night when all of a sudden another wolf howl echoed around the wood.

'Okay Andrew, give me back my twenty pound,' said Archie.

'Why?' asked Andrew.

'You killed the wrong wolf!'

A well-known Scottish proverb goes something like this:

'Money won't buy you happiness, but it will make the misery much easier to bear!'

An Englishman was driving through Fife when he collided with a car driven by a native of the town.

'Are you okay?' asked the Scotsman.

'Not too bad,' replied the Englishman. 'A bit shaken that's all.'

It was then the Scotsman produced a hip flask from an inside pocket.

'Here, would you like a wee dram of whisky to calm your nerves?' he said offering the flask.

The Englishman gratefully accepted and took a swig and handed it back to the Scotsman, who put the flask back in his pocket.

'Are you not having one?' the Englishman enquired.

'No, I'd rather not,' the Scotsman said. 'The police will be here soon!'

'Do you know that only half the bagpipe players who die go to heaven?' asked Hamish.

'Why's that?' asked Hector.

'Because,' Hamish began, 'if any more went it wouldn't be heaven!'

Three Scottish mice were having a chat one day.

'I'm so strong,' said the first mouse, 'that I can hold back the spring on a mousetrap and take the cheese.'

'Och get away,' said the second mouse. 'My body is so fit, that I could drink rat poison and not be affected.'

At that point the third mouse started to walk away.

'Where you going?' asked one of the other mice.

'I'm just nipping home to thump the cat!'

Hector McRector the burly rugby player from Pitlochry came home from a match with a torn ear, three broken teeth and a broken nose. His wife was understanding but told him that he should really give them back to the players he took them off!

The Scots aren't silly you know. When Hamish went to work on the building site for the first time the foreman said he had an intelligence question to ask him before he started work.

'So Hamish,' he said. 'It takes 20 men eight hours to build a wall 12 metres long and 3 metres high. How long would it take ten men?'

'Och, no time at all,' said Hamish.

'Why?' asked a puzzled foreman.

'Well, the 20 men have already built it!' replied Hamish.

Morag McPennyless was disturbed one night by a sound downstairs. When she went down she saw a burglar sneaking about in the dark.

'What are you doing?' she screamed.
The burglar turned and spoke,

'Stay back hen! I won't hurt you, but I'm hunting for all your money.'

'Well, switch the light on,' said Morag, 'and I'll hunt with you!'

The Minister had popped round to see Ol' Hughie and had noticed a bowl of almonds on the table.

'Those almonds look nice,' said the Minister.

'Och aye. My young grandson gave them to me as a present, but I dinnae want them,' replied Ol' Hughie. 'Help yourself.'
The Minister, who was fond of almonds, thanked Ol' Hughie and began to eat the nuts.

'I must admit Hughie, these seem a funny present to give to a man like yourself who has no teeth,' the Minister said between mouthfuls.

'Not really Reverend,' said Ol' Hughie. 'I like sucking the chocolate off them!'

Do you know there are cruel people out there who torture Scotsmen?

They tie their feet together, and then pick up the bagpipes and play a jig!

A Scotsman went into a jewellers to buy his wife a diamond ring. Unfortunately every ring the young female sales assistant showed him, he claimed was too expensive. After many rings the Scotsman said to the assistant,

'Can you no show me something cheap?'

'Have you tried looking in a mirror?' replied the sales assistant.

An old Scotsman was in his late nineties when the undertaker approached him and asked if he would like to make any arrangements for when he passed away, such as making money available for his funeral.

'Och no,' said the old Scotsman. 'I could be lost at sea!'

Did you hear the one about the Scotsman who was going to become an atheist?

He gave the idea up when he found out there were no holidays!

Farmer McDonald turned down a very large sum of money from a Scottish Train Company who wanted to build a new railway line across his land and through his barn. Farmer McDonald was asked by reporters why he, a Scotsman, had turned down such a substantial amount of money.

'Och, I dinnae like the idea of having to go down to the barn to open and shut the doors every time a train was coming through.'

A snooty Scottish lady went into a department store and said to the girl at the glove department,

'I say, young lady, I would like to purchase some fur gloves.'

'What fur?' asked the girl.

'What fur?' snorted the lady. 'Och, fur me hands of course!'

Ewan and Molly were lovestruck teenagers and had decided to get married. At the service the minister asked Ewan to repeat after him,
'All my worldly goods, I give to you.'
Ewan's mum turned to her husband and said,
'There goes his paper round!'

Big Tam was up before the judge again on a drunk and disorderly charge.
'This is the seventh time you've stood before me this year,' said the judge. 'And for being such a habitual offender I shall fine you on this occasion £500. Do you have anything to say?'
Big Tam looked at the judge and said,
'Will you no give me a wee discount for being a regular customer?'

Hamish always closed his eyes when he drank whisky. Why? Well, his doctor told him that he should never look at whisky again!

Rory and Wallace were playing a round of golf on one of Scotland's most notorious and mountainous highland courses. Having just played out of a very, very deep ravine Rory joined Wallace back on the fairway.

'How many was that?' asked Wallace.

'Three,' replied Rory.

'But I heard six,' Wallace said.

'Three were echoes!' Rory answered.

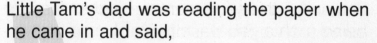

Little Tam's dad was reading the paper when he came in and said,

'Dad, will you take me to the zoo tomorrow?'

Without looking up from his paper, Little Tam's dad replied,

'No. If the zoo wants you, let them come and get you!'

A piper was practising very badly late one night when there was a knock on the front door. He opened it and was confronted by a very angry neighbour.

'Do you know we have a young baby next door?' demanded the neighbour.

'No,' said the piper. 'But if you start singing it, I may be able to improvise something!'

The building site foreman stopped Archie and asked him why he was only carrying one plank of wood while all the other workers were carrying two?

'Well,' said Archie, 'I guess they're all too bone idle to do two trips like me!'

MacDougal was a very resourceful Scotsman. Once his wife had a temperature of 105 degrees Fahrenheit, so he put her in the cellar to heat the house!

Two elderly Scottish couples were enjoying a cup of tea at the day centre when one husband turned the other and asked,

'So how is that "Improve your memory" course going for you down at that clinic?'

'Och it's great,' said the other husband. 'They teach all sorts of things there, all geared to improve your memory, like word association for example. It's working well.'

'And what's the name of this clinic?' asked the first husband.

The second husband thought for a while and then said,

'Hold on, I can do this.'

He closed his eyes and seemed to be in deep thought, then he asked,

'What's the name of the wild flower that grows in the glens? It has purple flowers and is very bushy.'

'You mean heather?' said the first husband.

'Aye, that's it,' smiled the second husband as he turned to his wife and said, 'Heather, what is the name of that clinic we go to?'

A young lassie was taking the collection during a church service and she approached Ol' Hughie.

'A pound for our Lord?' she asked.

'How old are you, lassie?' asked Ol' Hughie.

'I'm 16,' replied the girl.

'Well I'm 92,' said Ol' Hughie. 'I'll probably be seeing him sooner than you, so I'll give it to Him myself!'

The judge is summing up a divorce case.

'Mr Anderson, I have looked at the case notes and the implications very carefully regarding this divorce, and I have decided to award your ex-wife the sum of £600 per month.'

'Thanks very much, your honour,' smiled Anderson. 'I'll tell you what, I might even see if I could send her a few quid a month myself as well.'

A tipsy Englishman stood up in a Scottish bar and addressed the drinkers within.

'I was born an Englishman,' he bellowed, 'I was raised an Englishman, I married a Englishwoman and I shall die an Englishman.'

It was then a Scotsman stood up at the back and shouted back,

'Hoots mon, have ye no ambition?'

A Scotsman was in London and was amazed by the amount of pigeons flying around.

'Och, what do those birds live on?' he asked his English friend.

'Oh, scraps of food that people throw away,' said his friend.

'I see,' said the Scotsman. 'I wonder why we don't get birds like that in Scotland?'

A Scotsman had invited his friend to a party.

'You know where I live, don't you?' he said. 'It's up the high street, past the petrol station, left at the bookies and down that street to the corner, then it's the fourth house on the right, down the next street. Just ring the bell with your elbow.'

'Why would I ring your doorbell with my elbow?' asked his friend.

'Well you'll no be coming empty-handed now will ye?' replied the Scotsman!

No one knew why, but Dougal was intent on learning to play the bagpipes. One night he was stomping around in his size nine boots, piping for all his worth.

'Och, Dougal!' shouted his wife. 'That's an awful noise you're making.'

'Oh I'm sorry, hen,' said Dougal. 'I'll take my boots off.'

Maggie and Archie were sitting down to breakfast one morning when Maggie said,

'Oh Archie, I had the most wonderful dream last night. I dreamt that you bought me a beautiful diamond ring and took me on a world cruise. What do you think it could mean?'

Archie looked at her and smiled,

'Och, hen you'll find out tonight.'

Maggie was so excited during the day that she could hardly wait for Archie to come home that evening. When he did arrive he had a beautifully wrapped present under his arm. Maggie excitedly unwrapped it and there in a box was a book on the meaning of dreams!

Did you hear the one about the famous Scottish golfer?

He finally gave up playing the game after thirty years. He lost his ball!

An Irishman was up before the judge on a drunk and disorderly charge and was asked where he had bought the two bottles of whisky that had resulted in his behaviour.

'I didn't buy them,' said the Irishman. 'A Scotsman bought them for me.'
The judge sentenced the Irishman to fourteen days in prison for perjury!

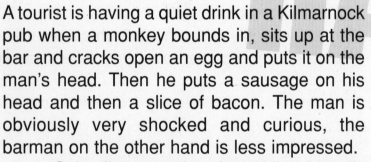

A tourist is having a quiet drink in a Kilmarnock pub when a monkey bounds in, sits up at the bar and cracks open an egg and puts it on the man's head. Then he puts a sausage on his head and then a slice of bacon. The man is obviously very shocked and curious, the barman on the other hand is less impressed.

'Och, dinnae worry about him,' he tells the man. 'He thinks he's a griller!'

Pat went round to Paddy's house and was surprised to see a set of bagpipes in the living room.

'Bought some bagpipes, Paddy?'

'No,' said Paddy. 'I borrowed from the Scotsman next door.'

'But you can't play the bagpipes,' said Pat.

'And neither can he while I have them!' smiled Paddy.

'Och doctor,' said a worried Archie down the phone to the Doctor. 'Could you come round and see Maggie as soon as possible? She's no well. I even had to carry her downstairs to make my dinner!'

Did you hear about the gang of silly Scottish bank-thieves?

They broke into the Bank of Scotland and deposited £750,000!

It's a well-known fact that an Irishman laughs at a joke at least three times:
Once when everybody he is with, gets it;
the second time a week later when he thinks he gets it;
and the third time a month later when the Scotsman explains it to him!

NEWSFLASH!
Chaos ensued in parts of Scotland today when a number of people ran out into the streets holding aloft empty whisky tumblers. Apparently they had heard on the weather report that there was going to be a nip in the air!

'Well Mr McCready,' said Dr Kilpatrick. 'I can examine you for ten pounds.'
　　'Ten pounds? Och doctor, that's great. if you find any, you can have one!'

An English yokel, an Irish yokel, and a Scottish yokel were leaning on a farm gate looking into a field at a cow.

'Now there's a fine specimen of an English cow,' said the English yokel. 'You can tell by its fine coat.'

'No it's not,' the Irish yokel disagreed. 'Look at that hard-working tail keeping all the flies away. That's an Irish cow.'

'You're both wrong,' said the Scottish yokel. 'It's a Scottish cow.'

'How can you tell?' asked the English yokel.

'Just look at that fine set of bagpipes it's got underneath its belly!'

A Scotsman was being interviewed for a job.

'So you start on £19,000 and then get £21,000 six months later,' said the employer.

'In that case,' said the canny Scot, 'I'll start in six months time.'

On their way to a big match at Hampden Park four Englishmen got on a train just behind four Scots, who the Englishmen had noticed had only bought one ticket between them. When the ticket collector was approaching, the four Scotsmen went off to the toilet and the Englishmen watched as they all piled in to one cubicle and locked the door. The ticket collector arrived at the cubicle, knocked on the door and called, 'Ticket Please.' One of the Scotsmen pushed their only ticket under the door, and the ticket collector punched it and slid it back under the door. When he was gone, the Scotsmen came out of the cubicle and went back to their seat. This had really impressed the English who decided that they would do the same on the return trip.

So the four Englishmen bought just one ticket and sat with the same Scotsmen as before whom they now noticed hadn't bought any tickets at all. When the ticket collector approached once again the Scotsmen all piled into one cubicle and this time the Englishmen all got into the cubicle next to them. When the Englishmen had closed their door, one of the Scots leaned out of their cubicle, banged on the Englishmen's door and called, 'Ticket please.' When the ticket appeared under the door, one of the Scotsmen took it and quickly closed the cubicle door!

Hector was in hospital and Hamish had come to visit him.

'So what's it like here?' Hamish asked.

'Oh it's no bad,' said Hector. 'The nurses are very nice and the treatment is good, but the food… Oh Hamish the food is so boring. We get haggis for breakfast, haggis for lunch, haggis for dinner and even get haggis for supper.'

'Well what do you expect laddie?' Hamish said. 'This is the Burns Unit.'

It's not very well known that a Scottish film company was going to make the sequel to *The Silence Of The Lambs*.

They were going to call it *Shut Up Ewes Two!*

A bagpiper had just finished murdering *Flower of Scotland* in a pub one night and asked the locals if they would like him to play something else. Someone at the bar called back,
    'How about darts?'

Hefty Morag-May pops into a fish and chip shop and asks for ten Mars bars in batter.
    'Is that all for you?' says the assistant behind the counter.
    'Och no!' says Morag-May. 'Me boyfriend will want one!'

'I'm sorry Big Tam,' said the optician, 'but you're going to have to wear glasses at work.'
    'Och that's going to be a bit of a wee problem,' replied Big Tam.
    'Why's that?' asked the optician.
    'I'm a boxer,' said Big Tam.

'So why did you come back early from your holidays?' Mac asked Frazer.

'Well I took the family to stay on a farm just outside Invergordon,' began Frazer. 'It was lovely wee place, but on the first day a sheep died and we had lamb for dinner. The next day a cow died and we had beef for dinner and on the third day a pig died and we had bacon for dinner. Then on the fourth day the farmer's wife died, so we thought we'd skip dinner and come home.'

'Of course you know the difference between a singles bar and the circus?' Moira asked Maggie as they shared a glass of wine and a gossip.

'No, what's that?' asked Maggie.

'Well, the clowns don't come up and talk to you at the circus.'

In school one day, Wullie was asked a question by his teacher,

'If you had £10 and you multiplied it by ten, what would you get?'

'A new bike!' replied Wullie.

'So how did your trip to London go?' Douglas asked Cameron when they met.

'Aye it was great. I took one shirt and a ten-pound note and came home without having to change either!'

Ancient warrior, Big Hamish McScary the Red, roared to his battle-scarred compatriot,

'Why is Boadicea no fighting with us today?'

'She wisna' Pict!' his compatriot screamed back.

Did you hear the one about the Scotsman who bought his wife a long-lasting Christmas present?

He bought her a 5-year diary!

Not many people know that there is a Scottish businessman who donates vast amounts of money to charities and good causes. The reason nobody knows about him is because he likes to remain anonymous. He is so shy he won't even sign his name on the cheques he donates!

How do you keep a crofter busy for hours?

Put him in front of a mirror and tell him to wait for the other crofter to smile!

A Scottish football fan was arrested today when he threw a coin at the referee during a football match. Police caught him when he went up to the referee at the end of the match and asked for his penny back!

A fire had broken out at the headquarters of the Scottish national football team.

'Quick, save the cups!' screamed the manager.

'Och don't panic Boss,' replied his number 2. 'The fire is nowhere near the canteen.'

Rory walked into the pub with a little Scottie dog under his arm.

'What a nice looking wee dog,' said the barman.

'Och aye,' smiled Rory. 'I got it for the wife.'

'That's no a bad swap,' replied the barman.

A Scotsman in a London pub ordered a pint of beer. When he was served with it, he asked,

'Do you think you could get a wee nip of whisky in that?'

'Of course, Jock.' smiled the barman.

'Well in that case, fill it up with beer ye tight Sassenach!' growled the Scotsman.

A man went to see the Scottish fortune-teller Seymore Clearly and asked how much it would cost.

'Five pounds for one question.'

'Five pounds!' the man exclaimed. 'That's very expensive isn't it?'

'Next!' said the fortune-teller.

A piper suddenly remembered that he had left his set of bagpipes on the back seat of his car which he had not locked. He rushed back to the car park, opened the back door and found that someone had put another set of bagpipes on the back seat!

Tight Tam went in to see his boss Mr Ferguson.

'Er, Boss can I have the day off tomorrow? The wee wifey wants to go shopping.'

'Certainly not,' says Mr Ferguson.

'Oh thank you very much,' smiles Tam. 'You're a very kind man.'

How does Scotland's worst shepherd count his sheep?

'One sheep. Two sheep. Three sheep. Another one, another one, another...'

Firemen had to rescue a Scotsman from the roof of a pub the other day when he got stuck. When asked why he was up on the roof, he told the firemen that the barman had said that there were free drinks on the house!

Rory received a call on his mobile phone from his wife who was in a very bad way.

'Och Rory,' she screamed down the phone. 'I'm driving the car. The brakes have gone and I'm hurtling down a hill at 70 miles per hour. Oh Rory, what shall I do?'

'Okay hen, just calm down,' said Rory, 'dinnae worry and try not to crash into anything expensive!'

An Englishman, an Irishman and a Scotsman went for an afternoon out together. The Englishman spent £80, the Irishman spent £50 and the Scotsman spent a very enjoyable afternoon!

An Edinburgh taxi driver was really excited when he picked up Pamela Anderson from the airport. She looked so gorgeous that on the journey back into Edinburgh he could hardly keep his eyes on the meter!

Did you hear the one about Scotland's worst vet?

He couldn't give cats injections or tablets. Well, who's ever heard of a Scotsman putting anything *into* a kitty?

Willie Spendit was so mean with his money, that he would never spend any of it on trips to the seaside. But, he liked feeding the seagulls so he flushed some bread down the toilet!

NEWSFLASH!
Wullie Buyit, Scotland's tightest man was run over by a brewery lorry yesterday.
It was the first and last time that the drinks had been on him!

A Scotsman stood on a new set of computerised weighing scales. They not only told the person's weight but also something about their personality. The Scotsman put in his money and stood on the scales. The computer flashed and buzzed and then on the screen the message read:

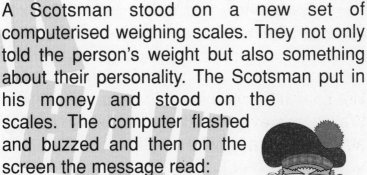

    'You are a tee–total sober spendthrift with a generous nature.'
It got his weight wrong too!

A Scottish fisherman by the name of Cast McFly was bragging about the 16-pound salmon he had recently caught.

'Och what a whopper!' exclaimed his friend. 'Did anyone see you land it?'

'Oh aye,' said McFly. 'Otherwise it would have weighed thirty-six pounds!'

A Highlander was queuing up at the ticket office in a train station.

'I'd like a return ticket please, laddie.'

'Where to? asked the ticket sales man.

'Back here, you stupid laddie!' replied the Highlander.

You always know when a Scotsman has paid you a compliment.

He asks for a receipt!

'I hear you have a new scarecrow,' said Farmer MacDonald to his neighbour Farmer Hehighhehihoe.

'Aye,' said the farmer.

'Is it scary?' asked MacDonald.

'Scary? Och it's scary alright,' replied Hehighhehihoe. 'Not only has it stopped the crows from stealing my corn, but they're bringing back what they nicked last year!'

Maggie phoned her husband and said,

'Dougal, I have some good news and some bad news about the car.'

'Oh aye,' said Dougal. 'What's the good news?'

'The airbags work,' replied Maggie.

129

The train stopped at the highland station and the tourist got off to stretch his legs.

'Ah, smell that Highland air,' he said to a nearby porter as he took a deep breath. 'Invigorating isn't it?'

The puzzled porter looked at him and said,

'Och no, it's Invergordon.'

Two drunk Scots wanted to pay their last respects to an old friend who had died recently. They stumbled into the funeral parlour and in their drunken state one of them fell over a piano.

'Och I've found the coffin,' slurred one of the drunks.

'Aye great, is it MacDougal's?' asked the other.

'I dinnae think so,' burped the first drunk 'but whoever it is, he has a fine set of teeth!'

Archie was sitting alone in the bar nursing a pint of heavy and looking very sad.

'What's up Archie?' asked the barman. 'You seem a bit down.'

'Aye I am,' sighed Archie. 'Me and the wife had a blazing row and she said that she wasn't going to talk to me for a whole month.' Thinking about Archie's wife, the barman looked at Archie and asked,

'Surely you should be happy about that?'

'I was,' sobbed Archie, 'but the month is up today!'

A pilot was flying in a hot air balloon and was lost somewhere over the Highlands. He looked down and saw a crofter out in a field and shouted,

'Hello there, can you tell me where I am?'

The crofter looked up.

'Where are ye? You're in the air!'

After extolling the virtues of Scotland all night in a pub in London, a bored Englishman talked to the boastful Scot.

'Look Jimmy, if Scotland is so good, why didn't you stay up there?'

'Well,' said the Scot, 'they're all so clever up there I had to come down here to have any chance of making it at all.'

Young Scottish lovers Cameron and Rhona were cuddling on the sofa one night when Rhona said,

'Do you know Cameron? We're just like Romeo and Juliet.'
Cameron smiled.

'Because we are intense lovers with only eyes for each other?'

'No,' said Rhona. 'My dad says if he catches us together he's going to kill you.'

Cameron took his girlfriend Rhona for a ride on his motorbike. As they rode along they passed a kebab wagon.

'Those kebabs smell nice, Cameron,' said a hopeful and hungry Rhona as they passed by.

'They certainly do,' said Cameron, turning the motorbike around. 'I'll drive a little closer so you can get a better smell.'

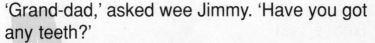

'Grand-dad,' asked wee Jimmy. 'Have you got any teeth?'

'I'm afraid not laddie,' said wee Jimmy's grand-dad with a toothless smile.

'Oh good,' said the young lad. 'Then you can hold my bag of sweets while I go out to play.'

Archie was six hours late back from the golf course and Maggie wasn't too pleased.

'*Where* have you been?' she snapped at Archie.

'Oh hen, it was terrible. I was playing with Billy, when on the 9th green he dropped dead. Twelve feet from the pin and my best friend dropped dead!'

'Och I'm sorry Archie,' apologised his wife. 'That's terrible!'

'It was, hen. All day it's been hit the ball... drag Billy. Hit the ball... drag Billy!'

Rhona went into the meat section in her local supermarket and asked for a leg of lamb. The butcher showed her a prime cut and she asked,

'Is it Scotch?'

'Why?' asked the butcher. 'Are you going to eat it or drink it?'

A Scotsman was arguing with a ticket collector on the Edinburgh to Dundee train over the price of a ticket. At one point the argument got so heated that the conductor took the Scotsman's suitcase and was about to throw it out of the window as the train passed over the Tay Bridge.

'Hoots man!' screamed the Scotsman. 'Not only are you trying to overcharge me, but now you're trying to drown my wee boy?'

Cameron had finally plucked up the courage to go round and see Rhona's dad and ask if he could marry his daughter.

'Would you still marry Rhona if she dinnae have any money?' asked Rhona's dad.

'Of course,' said Cameron eagerly.

'Then away with you,' said Rhona's dad. 'We've got enough idiots in the family as it is.'

The Highlands had never seen a winter like it. It had been non-stop snow blizzards and the Scottish recluse Herman McHermit hadn't been seen in the village for a very long time, so a Red Cross team were sent to his remote and tiny croft up in the mountains. When the rescue team finally got there, all they could see of McHermit's croft was the chimney poking out through the snow. Just to make sure that McHermit was still alive, one of the rescuers climbed up to the chimney and shouted down,

'McHermit, are you there?'

'Who's that?' called McHermit.

'It's the Red Cross!' the rescuer shouted back.

'Go away!' bellowed McHermit. 'I gave you a donation last year!'

Did you hear the one about the silly crofter?

He used to feed his chickens malt whisky so they would lay scotch eggs!

'So where did you meet your wife?' Tam asked Willie as they supped their ale in a local bar.

'In the Tunnel of Love,' replied Willie.

'Och, that's nice,' smiled Tam.

'Not really,' sighed Willie. 'She was digging it at the time!'

'I'm worried about my wife's appearance,' said Jimmy as he and Tam were having a drink in their local bar 'The Drunk and Disorderly'.

'Why's that?' asked Tam.

'I haven't seen her for three days!' sighed Jimmy.

Poor wee Gordy, he was such an ugly laddie, when he went to Edinburgh Zoo, he had to buy two tickets. One to get in and one to get out!

A tourist had just enjoyed a sumptuous meal in an Edinburgh restaurant and was paying the bill.

'I'm very sorry,' he said to the Scottish waiter as he counted out his cash, 'but I only have enough money for the bill. So I won't be able to leave a tip.'

'Och dinnae worry Sir,' smiled the waiter. 'Let me just add up your bill again.'

Why did the Australians invent the boomerang and not the Scots?

Well, who ever heard of a Scot throwing something away?

What's the difference between a bagpiper and a haggis?

Lots of people like haggis!

A tourist was sheltering in a doorway looking at the torrential rain as it fell on Edinburgh castle.

'I just don't believe this weather,' the tourist said to a nearby local. 'I've been here two weeks and all it's done is rain. When do you have a summer here?'

'It's hard to say,' answered the local. 'Last year it was on a Thursday.'

What's the difference between a set of bagpipes and an onion?

No one cries when you chop up a set of bagpipes!

Scotland's most famous actor and actress husband and wife team, Shelly and Kenneth McLovies were at home one day when Shelly called out,

'Kenneth, where are you?'

'I'm in the kitchen hen,' Kenneth called back.

'Oh can I be in it too?' pleaded Shelly.

'Well we've won the lottery! Life will never be the same again, hen,' said Wallace to his wee wifey Wendy.

'Och that's true,' grinned Wendy. 'But what about the begging letters?'

'Oh, we'll keep sending them,' replied her husband!

NEWSFLASH!

It's been discovered through historical research why Scotsmen wear kilts. Apparently in 1311 Douglas McAdam won a lady's tartan skirt in a raffle!

Old Fraser was sitting fishing on the banks of the Clyde when a passer by stopped to chat.

'So how many fish have you caught today?'

'Well,' said Fraser, 'if I catch this one I'm trying for, plus another three, that'll be four in all.'

Henpecked husband Hughie McWeddie had been married to Scotland's most house-proud wife for many, many years, but got the last laugh when he died. His last request was to have his ashes scattered over her carpet.

The Loch Ness Monster popped into a local bar near the loch and ordered a pint of heavy.

'That'll be thirty pounds,' said the barman and added, 'I would have never believed that you would walk into my bar for a drink.'

'At your prices I'm no surprised!' growled Nessie.

'Oh Cameron,' sighed Rhona as they snuggled up close on the sofa. 'Kiss me.'
So Cameron gave her a long lingering romantic kiss.

'Oh Cameron,' sighed Rhona again. 'Whisper in my ear, those three magic words I love to hear you say.'
So Cameron leant towards her ear and whispered,

'Money, Money, Money.'

'I hear Ol' Hughie was killed the other day,' Sandy told Tam.

'Och, that's a shame. What happened?' asked Tam.

'He was drinking milk,' said Sandy.

'Drinking milk?' Tam said in surprised tones. 'How on earth could the man die from drinking milk?'

'The cow fell on him!' replied Sandy.

Did you hear about the old Scotsman who sold his gold watch to his only son from his deathbed? Did you also hear that the son paid him with a post-dated cheque?

MacDonald stood before the judge on a petty crime charge.

'Haven't I seen you before, Mr MacDonald?' asked the judge.

'Aye, my lord. I gave your daughter bagpipe lessons.'
The judge then gave MacDonald thirty years!

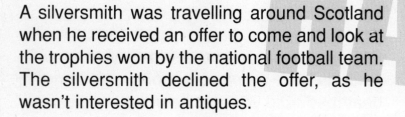

A silversmith was travelling around Scotland when he received an offer to come and look at the trophies won by the national football team. The silversmith declined the offer, as he wasn't interested in antiques.

Did you hear the one about why the fifty pence piece is such an unusual shape?

So that you can get it out of a Scotsman's fist with an adjustable spanner!

'Now listen Frazer,' said the doctor. 'You're either going to have to give up drinking whisky or go blind. It's your choice.'

Old Frazer thought for a while then sighed.

'Well doctor, I'm a old man,' he said. 'I think that I've seen just about everything that's worth seeing!'

Having got over the trauma of actually buying two raffle tickets, Big May found out that one of her tickets won the £5,000 cash prize.

'Och, that grand!' said Wee Mary.

'Not really,' moaned Big May. 'I'm very disappointed.'

'Disappointed!' said an amazed Wee Mary. 'Why on earth are you disappointed?'

'Well my second ticket dinnae win anything!'

145

Andrew had just been out for the evening with a young lassie and when he arrived home his dad said to him,

'I hope this young lassie isn't costing you too much money?'

'Not at all dad,' replied Andrew. 'In fact tonight only cost £10.'

'Aye that's no bad,' said Andrew's dad, relieved.

'Well it's all she had!' smiled Andrew.

Two not too bright Scots were in London when they saw a very grand building with a corner stone that had the Roman Numerals MCMIV etched into it.

'Will ye look at that Angus?' said one of the Scotsmen. 'One of the finest buildings in London and a Scotsman has got his name on it!'

Did you hear the one about the Scotsman who was so mean that he wouldn't buy an address book?

He got a telephone directory and crossed out the names and addresses of the people he didn't know!

Maggie came back from the doctors and told Archie that the doctor had said that she wasn't too well and should rest and maybe take in some ocean breeze. So Archie, being the dutiful Scottish husband he was, sat her down, and fanned her with a herring.

Did you hear the one about the Scotsman who was arrested?

He vowed he'd never wipe sweat from his forehead with the hem of his kilt again!

Maggie was getting a little bored with her marriage to Archie, as he never took her out. One night, while he was reading the newspaper, Maggie asked him a question,

'Archie, what would it take you to go on a second honeymoon?'

Without looking up from his newspaper, Archie replied,

'A second wife!'

The McDougals had just had a lovely meal round at the McFrugals' and Mr McFrugal suggested that they all partake in a coffee in the library. Unfortunately by time they drove to the library it was closed!

Andy McThug is Scotland's worst football hooligan. He's the only man who goes to a football match and buys two tickets for two seats. One to sit in and one to throw!

Jeanie and Archie were a very talkative couple and a guide, who was going to take them climbing in the Highlands, knew it. So he came up with a plan.

'Look you two,' he said, 'mountain climbing takes a lot of concentration and that means no talking. So what I'm going to do is charge you ten pounds every time either of you talk while we're out climbing.'

Jeanie and Archie agreed and spent a wonderful day scaling one of the most picturesque and dangerous mountains in the Highlands. When they reached the summit the mountain climber said to Jeanie,

'Well here we are and tell me, were you ever tempted to speak at all?'

'Only once,' said Jeanie.

'When was that?' asked the climber.

'When Archie fell over the edge!'

Hamish was filling in an application form while Hector looked on.

'What do you think I should put here?' asked Hamish.

'What's the question?' Hector replied.
'Please give details of the person to notify in the case of an emergency,' Hamish read out.

'Well,' said Hector, 'I always put down "The nearest doctor".'

'Do you know what Wee Scottie?' the big barman said. 'You must be the most henpecked man in Scotland.'

'Och, come on now,' squeaked Wee Scottie. 'You wouldnae say that to me if my wife was here!'

Angus D. Expense was an accountant and was looking for a computer for his business.

'This is a fantastic computer,' said the store assistant. 'It's so powerful, it will do half your job for you.'

So Angus bought two!

A Glaswegian walks into a cake shop and asks in his very, very thick accent,

'That cake in the window – is it a macaroon, or a meringue?'

The woman behind the counter looks in the window then replies,

'No you're right, it's a macaroon!'

A Scotsman drank so much whisky when he was in America on holiday, that his wife had to pay duty on him to get him through Edinburgh airport customs!

A Scotsman drowned today when he fell into vat of whisky. Police forensics experts said that it had, unfortunately, been a slow death as the man had to get out of the vat twice to go to the toilet!

NEWSFLASH!
Police were called to a rough tenement block when a man was badly injured in a fight over a carpet. Police believe that the incident may be rug-related!

Two old dears were chatting over a cup of tea and a slice of Dundee cake in a Scottish tearoom.

'I see they've reduced the bus fare for senior citizens,' said one old girl.

'I know. It's disgusting,' said the other old girl. 'I used to save twenty pence by not using the bus, now I only save fifteen!'

Hamish, worst for drink, was staggering down the road very late one night when a patrol car pulled alongside and the policeman asked,

'And where are you off to, pal?'

'A lecture,' slurred Hamish.

'Oh sure,' said the policeman. 'And who is going to give a lecture this time of night?'

'The wife!' moaned Hamish.

'Doc, I dinnae know what's the matter with me recently,' said a worried MacTavish. 'Some days I just don't know where I am at all?'

'Fares please!' shouted the bus conductor.

Old Scotty died and being a typical Scot his will began:

'Being of sound mind, I put all my money in the bank!'

153

A policeman on his rounds could tell that the two Scots outside the pub were very drunk. For a start one of them was throwing five pound notes away and the second one was picking them up and handed them back to him.

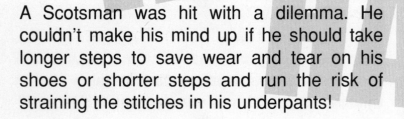

A Scotsman was hit with a dilemma. He couldn't make his mind up if he should take longer steps to save wear and tear on his shoes or shorter steps and run the risk of straining the stitches in his underpants!

To give you some idea as to how wet the Isle of Skye is, a tourist once asked a local how far Dunvegan Castle was from Portree and got this reply:

'About 18 mile as the crow swims!'

A Scottish doctor gave a patient six months to live. At the end of the six months the patient still hadn't paid the doctor's bill, so the doctor gave him another six months!

It was Christmas time and to celebrate Hamish poured his friend, Hector, a tiny, tiny glass of whisky.

'There you are Hector. That's a 15-year-old whisky.'

'Is it now?' said Hector looking at the miniscule measure. 'It's very small for its age!'

'Do you know why bagpipers march while they play?' Hector asked Hamish as they shared a cup of tea and a scone at the tearoom.

'To get as far away from the noise as possible!' replied Hamish.

Morag McKinley from the Shetland Isles was invited down to Glasgow University by a professor who had heard that she could tell the species of certain wasps just by the buzz they made. He had made a record of wasp noises and began playing it to Morag, but unfortunately she couldn't recognise any. The professor was shocked and disappointed. Then he looked at the record and apologised to Morag.

'I'm so sorry,' he said. 'No wonder you don't recognise the sounds on this record. I'm playing the Bee side!'

What is the difference is between a canoe and a Scotsman?

Well as you all know a canoe sometimes tips!

'How was the party your new Scottish boss threw the other evening?' Fred asked Bill.

'Oh it was a typical Scottish party,' replied Bill. 'The wine flowed like glue.'

'Och Hamish, that set of bagpipes are out of tune,' said Hector.

'How can you tell?'

'Because you're blowing into them!'

A man went into a Scottish fish and chip shop.

'Fish and chips twice, please.'

The woman behind the counter looked up from the frier.

'It's okay, I heard you the first time.'

Archie knew he had upset his wife when he arrived home one evening and she wasn't there.

There was a note that told him his salad was in the garden!

A Scottish wife went to see a psychiatrist about her husband.

'Och, doctor. He's in a bad way, he thinks he's a lift.'
The psychiatrist ponders this revelation for a moment then says,

'Well, this is very strange. I think the best thing to do is to get him to call in and see me.'

'Oh, he cannae do that doctor,' said the wife.

'Why not?' asked the psychiatrist.
'He disnae stop at this floor!'

Did you hear the one about the little Scottish boy who went to the cinema?

The girl on the ticket counter said that he couldn't get in because the film was an 18 and over only. He spent the rest of the afternoon finding 17 more friends to go with him!

Which is the odd one out? The Loch Ness Monster, a haggis or a silly Scot?

A haggis. The other two don't exist!

A Highlander visiting Edinburgh Zoo stood in front of the snake-house sticking his tongue out at all the snakes.

'What's going on here?' asked the keeper.

'Look here laddie,' said the Highlander. 'They started it!'

Did you hear the one about the Scotsman who threw away his water skis?

He couldn't find a river that sloped!

'Oh Archie, I'm think I'm losing my mind,' said Archie's wife.

'Och, I'm no surprised wee woman,' replied Archie. 'You've been giving me a piece of it every day for the last twenty years.'

I'm not saying that he was a typical Scotsman, but he had moths in his wallet that hadn't learnt to fly yet!

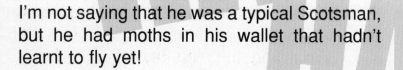

Paramedics treated a Scotsman for shock today when he was involved in an accident at a bank in Fife.

Apparently he got in the wrong queue and made a withdrawal!

Did you hear the one about the Scottish computer?

It saves everything, but won't tell you where it's put it!

A Scotsman rang the maternity ward and said excitedly,

'I'm going to bring my wife in. She's going to have a bairn.'

'Is this her first baby?' asked the nurse on the other end of the line.

'No,' said the Scotsman. 'It's her husband!'

A haggis walks in to a bar and orders a wee dram.

'Sorry,' said the barman. 'We don't serve food here.'

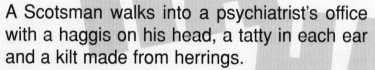

A Scotsman walks into a psychiatrist's office with a haggis on his head, a tatty in each ear and a kilt made from herrings.

'I can see you've got a problem,' said the psychiatrist.

'Aye that's true,' replied the Scotsman. 'I'm worried about my brother.'

Two Scots worst for drink are walking down a road in London.

'Is this Wembley?' asks the first Scot.

'Not it's Thursday,' replied his friend.

'So am I,' said the first Scot. 'Let's go for a drink.'

'I'm afraid to have to tell you, Mr McGregor,' said the doctor, 'but you have rabies.'

'Quick, get me a pen and paper,' replied McGregor.

'To write your will?'

'Och no,' grinned McGregor, 'I want to make a list of all the Sassenachs to bite.'

A Scottish family went to a local riding stable and the dad asked if he could hire a horse.

'Certainly Sir,' said the stable lad. 'What sort?'

'A big one,' said the dad, 'there's five of us!'

Wee Annie was sitting on the wall crying when a sweet old lady came up and asked her what was wrong.

'Och Missus,' Wee Annie said between sobs, 'I've lost my fifty pence piece.'

'Oh dear,' said the sweet old lady opening her purse. 'Now don't you cry. Look, here's fifty pence for you.'
The sweet old lady handed the money to Wee Annie who sobbed even louder.

'What's the matter now?' asked the sweet old lady.

'If I hadn't lost my fifty pence piece, I'd have a pound now,' bawled Wee Annie.

An overweight Irishman asked a Scotsman if it would be any good trying to borrow £20 from him?

'Aye, okay,' said the Scot. 'The wrestle and the exercise will do ye good!'

'My husband, Gregor suggested a candlelit dinner last night,' said Maggie.

'Och, that's so romantic,' sighed Jennie.

'Not really. It just saved him having to buy a new light bulb.'

There was a great party in the town. The Irishman brought Guinness. The Englishman brought beer, the Frenchman brought wine and the Scotsman brought his brother!

Hector went round to Hamish's house and found him stripping the wallpaper.

'Are you re-decorating?' asked Hector.

'Och no,' replied Hamish. 'I'm moving house.'

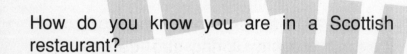

How do you know you are in a Scottish restaurant?

There's a fork in the sugar bowl and the knives are heated, so you don't use too much butter.

NEWSFLASH!
Two black taxis collided in Queen Street in Edinburgh. Two people were seriously injured but the other twenty escaped with just cuts and bruises!

Did you hear the one about the Scotsman who was too mean to buy stamps?

He sent his friend a homing pigeon for Christmas!

Hamish McHamish, the famous Scottish explorer was exploring the deepest and darkest areas of Africa when he came across a tribe gathered around a fierce looking Witch Doctor who was beating on a large set of drums.

'What are you doing?' asked Sir Hamish.

'We no water have,' growled the Witch Doctor.

'Ah I see,' said Sir Hamish. 'And I guess you are sending a message to the rain Gods?'

'No,' replied the Witch Doctor. 'Me calling a plumber.'

Archie and Maggie went to the dentist.

'Now listen here,' said Archie to the dentist.'I dinnae want to pay for any fancy needles or injections or gas, I just want you to pull the tooth out. I don't care how much it hurts, I just want it done as quickly and more importantly as cheaply as you can.'

'Not a problem,' said the dentist. 'What tooth is it?'

Archie turned to Maggie and said,
'Show him your bad tooth, hen!'

Did you hear about the Scotsman who took a baby alarm back to Mothercare?

He said it didn't work – his wife had a baby!

A Scotsman's theory on exercise:

If God had wanted us to touch our toes,
He would have put them on our knees!

Two priests were discussing Scottish weddings and one of them said,
'Of course you can always tell who the bride is at a crofters' wedding.'
'How?' asked the other.
'She's the one wearing the white wellington boots!'

A Scottish professor of telekinesis stood before a group of students in a Scottish university and asked,

'If there is anybody here who believes in telekinesis could they please raise my right hand?'

'Do you know there are over 300 pubs in Edinburgh and I haven't been in one of them?' boasted Big Tam one evening. Then added,

'I'll find it some day!'

Wee Jenny runs into her mummy and asks,

'Mummy, mummy, can I play with my doll's house please?'

'Och don't be silly hen. You know I rented it out to five Edinburgh art students.'

When a Scotsman and Scotswoman are wearing kilts at the same time, how do you tell which one is the man and which is the woman? The one in the kilt, listening, is the man!

'I had a brass band at my wedding,' Flora said to Moira.

'Och that's nice,' replied Moira.

'Not really,' Flora sighed. 'It was on my finger!'

'I love the sounds of the pipes,' said the proud Scotsman.

'Do you play the bagpipes?' asked a curious Irishman.

'No,' replied the Scot. 'I'm a plumber!'

'You Scots are a strange bunch,' an Englishman told his Scottish friend.

'What do you mean?' asked the Scot.

'Well in Scotland men eat oats, while in England we give it to our horses.'
The Scotsman looked at the Englishman and with a smile said,

'And that's why English horses and Scotsmen are the finest in the world!'

An American and a Scotsman were looking at the mighty Niagara Falls.

'Gee buddy, I bet you don't have anything like that in Scotland?' said the American.

'Och, no we don't,' replied the Scotsman, 'but I know a plumber in Dumbarton who could fix that.'

Hector was showing Hamish the rather dubious second-hand car he had just bought.

'It can do ninety,' said Hector proudly.

'Per hour, per litre or perhaps?' replied Hamish.

A Dunhaggis United supporter hands over his £50 at the turnstile at a home match and says,

'Two please.'

'Okay pal,' says the ticket man. 'Will that be for a Striker or a Defender?'

The haggis is an unusual dish. Most people are never sure whether to eat it or kick it. Then when they've eaten it, they wish they had kicked it!

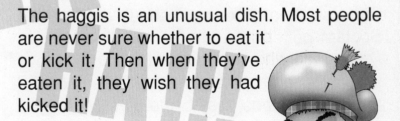

Did you hear the one about why Scottish families buy double-glazing?

To stop the bairns hearing the ice cream van when it comes around!

Did you hear the one about Scotland's toughest hotel?

To give you an idea as to how tough it is, the staff steal the customers' towels!

Did you hear the one about the terrible Scottish golfer?

He was so bad at the game that when he tried to grow tomatoes, they came up sliced!

Did you hear the one about Scotland's meanest man?

He was so mean that he saved all his toys for his second childhood!

'I was really surprised that I met my wife in a singles bar,' McDougall told McTavish.

'Why were you surprised?' asked McTavish.

'I thought she was at home looking after the bairns!'

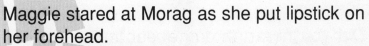

Maggie stared at Morag as she put lipstick on her forehead.

'Morag, what are you doing hen?' asked Maggie.

'My boyfriend is taking me out tonight and he said that I need to make my mind up.'

Mary went into her local butcher's shop in Arbroath to buy a chicken. It was late in the day and the butcher only had one chicken left.

'Will this one do?' asked the butcher.

'Och, it's a wee bit wee,' said Mary. 'Have ye no got something bigger?'

'Just a minute. I'll see what I've got out the back,' said the butcher. So he raced out the back of the shop with the chicken, grabbed his bicycle pump and pumped up the chicken so it looked bigger.

'How about this one?' he asked when he returned.

'Och that's fine,' said Mary. 'I tell ye what, give me the both of them!'

Did you hear the one about the resourceful Scotsman who has found a new use for old razor blades?

He shaves with them!

Did you hear the one about the Scotsman who bought his wife a rocket for her birthday?

She was over the moon!

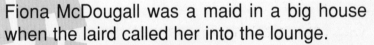

Did you know that in the olden days, the Scots used to play the bagpipes to frighten the English?

Now they just do it to annoy them!

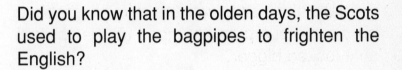

Fiona McDougall was a maid in a big house when the laird called her into the lounge.

'Fiona!' said the laird as he stood by the grand piano. 'Look at this piano, it's so dirty I could write my name in the dust.'

'Och Sir, smiled Fiona, 'that's education for you!'

177

A Scotsman walked into his local fishmonger's in Arbroath and said,

'I'd like a pair of Arbroath Smokies for the wife, please.'

'I'm sorry Sir, I dinnae have a pair left,' said the fishmonger.

'Och well, give me odd ones. She'll never notice!'

So what's the difference between a Scotsman and a coconut?

Well, you can get a drink out of a coconut!

Did you hear the one about the silly crofter who stood outside in his field for three days?

He thought he would win the Nobel Prize for being outstanding in his field!

'My doctor has told me to give up golf,' said Hector to his friend Hamish.

'Why? Has he seen your medical records?' asked Hamish.

'No. He's seen me play!' replied Hector.

Maggie and Moira were chatting over the garden fence.

'Och, I'm sorry to hear you buried your husband last week, Moira.'
Moira smiled weakly and replied,

'Aye, Maggie, I had to. He was dead!'

'I had a terrible row with the wife last night,' Hamish told Hector. 'But although she went on and on, I did manage to get the last word in.'

'Really?' asked Hamish.
'What did you say?'
Hamish sighed,

'"Okay!"'

Rory was worst for wear owing to one too many drams and went to see his doctor.

'Och Doc,' he moaned. 'Can you no give me something for me head?'

'Give you something?' laughed the doctor. 'I wouldnae take it if you were giving it away!'

'Can I interest you in this nice little pocket calculator?' asked the assistant in the Glasgow electrical shop where Angus, a thrifty Scotsman, was browsing.

'Och no,' replied Angus keeping a tight hold on his wallet. 'I already know how many pockets I've got.'

'Can you lend me £15?' Hector asked Hamish.

'But I only have £10,' Hamish replied. That's all right,' said Hector. 'You can owe me the other £5.'

Did you hear the one about the Scots girl who bought matching luggage for her honeymoon?

All the carrier bags came from the same supermarket!

Did you hear the one about the frugal Scotswoman?

She took off her glasses when she wasn't looking at anything so she wouldn't wear them out!

In Scotland there are two rules for drinking whisky.
Rule one: Never take whisky without water.
Rule two: Never take water without whisky!

Wee Jamie asked his Dad if he would like to save some money. His dad being a canny Scot said that he certainly would and what did his son suggest?

'Well Dad,' said Jamie. 'If you buy me a bike, I won't wear my shoes out so fast.'

A man runs into a Scottish pub and calls out.

'Has anyone lost a £100 note wrapped up with an elastic band?'
Big Jock puts up his hand.

'Great. I've got some good news for you. I've found the elastic band.'

Of course you know what a Scotsman calls six weeks of torrential rain?

Summer!

'Oh my bonny lass,' said Andrew to his date. 'Drink makes you look gorgeous.'

'But I havnae been drinking,' said his date.

'Oh, but I have,' smirked Andrew.

A wedding guest was chatting with Mr McTavish at his daughter's third wedding.

'Three times married, that must be bit of strain on you – organising three weddings.'

'Aye it is,' said McTavish, 'and the confetti is starting to get very dirty!'

'I went into town this morning to pay my gas bill,' Hamish told Hector, 'and I decided that I would pay it with a smile.'

'Aye that's nice,' said Hector.

'Not really,' sighed Hamish. 'The lassie behind the counter said that they would prefer the money!'

Two Scottish businessmen met and one said to the other,

'Business is very bad in this town.'

'I know,' said the other businessman, 'and I'm sorry to hear that your factory burned down.'

'Shhhh! That's tomorrow night!'

Did you hear the one about the Scotsman who took all his money out of his bank for a holiday?

After it had had a holiday, he put it all back in again!

Archie was visiting an aquarium when he fell into a tank of man-eating sharks. He managed to survive and get out unscathed due to the fact he was wearing a T-shirt that had 'Scotland for the World Cup' written across the front. Let's face it, not even sharks could swallow that!

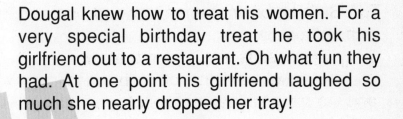

Dougal knew how to treat his women. For a very special birthday treat he took his girlfriend out to a restaurant. Oh what fun they had. At one point his girlfriend laughed so much she nearly dropped her tray!

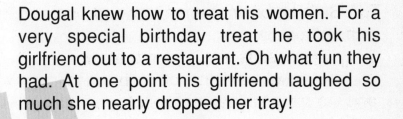

'Gee, did you know that that it takes three Highland sheep to make a cardigan?' said one American tourist to another.

'That's amazing!' said her friend. 'I didn't even know they could knit!'

The publishers of this fine book have received a complaint from a very angry Scotsman. Apparently he told them that if they didn't stop publishing jokes about Scotland and the Scots he would stop borrowing this book from his friend.

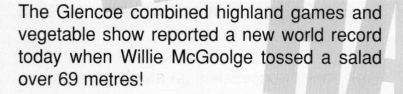

The Glencoe combined highland games and vegetable show reported a new world record today when Willie McGoolge tossed a salad over 69 metres!

Finlay won a toilet brush in a raffle and a few weeks later his friend Sandy asked him how he was getting on with it…

'Och, no much,' said Finlay, 'I've started using toilet paper again!

Wee Jock came home from school and asked his dad,

'Dad, is it true that I'm a descendant of apes?'

'Och I'm not sure,' said his dad. 'I don't know much about your mum's relatives!'

So what's the difference between a mean Scotsman and a tightrope?

Well think about it, at least a tightrope gives a little!

How do you stop a Cairn Terrier digging holes in the garden?

Easy! Hide his shovel!

What's the difference between the Scotland football team and a tea bag?

That's right, a tea bag stays in the cup longer!

A TV documentary had shown a couple of anglers in Scotland catching salmon, one holding the legs of the other while he dangled over a bridge, catching fish as they swam up river. Thinking this an excellent idea Jamie and Rab decided to try it themselves. They found a bridge and Rab dangled Jamie over. An hour passed when Jamie suddenly called,
'Quick! Pull me up quick!'
'Have you caught a salmon?' Rab said excitedly.
'No yet but there's a train coming!'

Did you hear the one about Wee Jamie spending a whole day in the library?

He was studying for a blood test!

Willie went to the doctors with splinters of glass in his mouth.

'Dear me Willie, how did that happen?' asked the doctor.

'I dropped me bottle of whisky on the floor and I dinnae want to waste it!' mumbled Willie.

'So you're looking for work, Mr McTavish?' said the man behind the desk at the job centre.

'Not necessarily,' replied McTavish 'but I'd like a job!'

There was a knock on a Scotsman's door one morning. When he opened it, a very angry neighbour confronted him.

'I left my house to go for a newspaper and that Scottie dog of yours went for me!' he snapped.

'He what? I've had that dog for ten years. I've fed him, walked him, looked after him and in all that time he's never *once* got the paper for me!'

Big Hughie was puzzled by something in the newspaper.

'Jamie, it says here that 8 out of 10 Scotsmen use ballpoint pens to write with.'

'So? said Jamie.

'Well,' asked a curious Big Hughie, 'what do the other two use them for?'

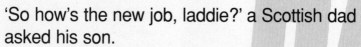

'So how's the new job, laddie?' a Scottish dad asked his son.

'I'm a Monback,' replied the young man.

The father looked confused. 'A Monback? What does a Monback do?'

'I work in a delivery warehouse, and when the lorries arrive, I stand behind them calling,

"Monback!"'

A Scotsman went to his local hospital with two badly scalded feet.

'How did that happen?' asked the nurse.

'I was heating up a tinned haggis,' said the Scotsman.

'But how did you burn your feet heating up a tinned haggis?'

'I dinnae know. I was only doing what it said on the tin,' replied the Scotsman. 'It said "after opening the tin, stand in boiling water for twenty minutes".'

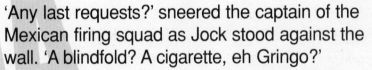

'Any last requests?' sneered the captain of the Mexican firing squad as Jock stood against the wall. 'A blindfold? A cigarette, eh Gringo?'

'No,' said Jock. 'I'd like to sing a song.'

'Very well, you sing your song, Scotsman, then we shoot you.' Jock took a deep breath and began to sing.

'40 millon green bottles standing on the wall, 40 millon green bottles standing on the wall...'

191

And finally...
The definition of a Scottish gentleman is someone who can play the bagpipes beautifully...but doesn't!